THE MODEL LEADER

A Fully Functioning Person

WILLIAM D. HITT

BATTELLE PRESS

Columbus • Richland

Library of Congress Cataloging-in-Publication Data

Hitt, William D.
    The model leader : a fully functioning person / by William D. Hitt.

        p.   cm.
    Includes bibliographical references and index.
    ISBN 0-935470-62-X : $24.95
    1. Leadership   I. Title
HD57.7.H58 1993
303.3'4—dc20   92-39347
                                                              CIP

Battelle Press
505 King Avenue
Columbus, Ohio 43201-2693
614-424-6393
1-800-451-3543
FAX: 614-424-5263

The process of becoming a leader is much the same as the process of becoming an integrated human being.

Warren Bennis

To my Grandchildren:

Jackie
Brian
Jessica
Brandon
Jake
Taylor

and all of my future grandchildren

ACKNOWLEDGMENTS

I was very fortunate in being able to enlist a Dream Team to review the manuscript before it went to press. For helping to remove the cataracts from my mind's eye, I give my heartfelt thanks to these team members: Grady Bogue, Bob Bowers, Neil Drobny, Cameron Fincher, Tom McClain, George Rieser, Charles St. John, Duane Sunderman, and Bill Wilkins.

For doing a superb job of editing the manuscript, I give my sincere thanks to Yvonne Burry. Yvonne's imprint can be found on every page of the book.

And for typing the manuscript, I thank Gwen Burton, Sherry Galford, and Jean Hayward. These three secretaries were able to take handwritten pages and turn them into beautiful text.

To each of you, I say "Thank you."

SPECIAL NOTES

On Language

The Model Leader is addressed to women and men alike. In my own writing, I try to be sensitive to gender. But some of the quotations included in the book may not adequately reflect a sensitivity to gender issues in leadership.

On Anecdotes

Each anecdote presented in the book is true in substance but not necessarily true in details. Some of the anecdotes have been altered slightly to protect the innocent.

CONTENTS

FOREWORD

$\mathscr{T}$he philosopher Immanuel Kant contrasted two different approaches to self-evaluation. He said one way is to compare yourself with an ideal of perfection and the second is to always be comparing yourself with other people. Kant stressed that the first approach is healthy and the second is not.

This book, by holding up for your view and examination a portrait of a model leader, can help you become a more effective leader. It begins with a general theory of leadership and then sets forth 25 specific leadership competencies. These competencies, taken collectively, describe the model leader. The term "model leader" will be used as an ideal type to designate the hypothetical individual who possesses all 25 competencies in full measure. The term "effective leader" will be used to designate the real-world person who is striving to become a model leader. This latter individual is the person to whom the book is addressed.

Perhaps no one in history has ever completely achieved the ideal as presented here—and perhaps no one in the future ever will—but this book can serve as a beacon on your journey.

I encourage you to read the book, reflect on what is being said, and complete the Leadership Agenda in the appendix. If you will then implement the Leadership Agenda over the next year or so, the probability is very high that you will be a more effective leader.

—Bill Hitt

THE MODEL LEADER

A Fully Functioning
Person

CHAPTER

I

A THEORY OF LEADERSHIP

If there was ever a moment in history when a comprehensive strategic view of leadership was needed, not by a few leaders in high office but by large numbers of leaders in every job, from the factory floor to the executive suite, from a McDonald's fast-food franchise to a law firm, this is certainly it.

Warren Bennis and Burt Nanus
Leaders

*K*urt Lewin, the well known social psychologist, never tired of saying, "There is nothing so practical as a good theory." Many practicing managers, however, view theory as academic, unrealistic, and impractical. These managers are concerned with the world of hard knocks and the bottom line. They don't have time to think about such lofty notions as conceptual frameworks, postulates, corollaries, and hypotheses.

But Lewin was right. What is needed is a good theory of leadership. Such a theory can serve as a road map; it can be a directional tool for leaders. A good theory will:

- *Be consistent with the facts.* There have been scores of leadership studies that have generated empirical data. Assuming the data have been verified, then any theory must be consistent with these data.

- *Help explain the facts.* Given the distinction between data (facts) and information (meaningful data), a good theory will help translate data into information.

- *Have predictive power.* By focusing on cause-and-effect relationships, a good theory will predict with some degree of accuracy that when A and B occur, C will follow.

- *Be useful to practitioners.* Many theoreticians who are reasonably effective can communicate with other theoreticians, but are unable to communicate with practitioners. (In fact, some are not even interested in communicating with practitioners.) But in the field of leadership, one's theories must be understood by practitioners. Otherwise, the theories will simply remain on the shelf to collect dust.

This book proposes a theory of leadership that meets these four criteria. It is intended for two particular audiences: practicing managers who want to become effective leaders and students of leadership who aspire to become effective leaders.

This chapter provides a conceptual framework—a general outline of an effective leader. The following chapters discuss in detail five dimensions of leadership, each with its specific leadership competencies. The total list of 25 competencies describes the model leader.

The Leadership Jungle

If Lewin is correct, shouldn't there be such a thing as a universal theory of leadership—one that can be adopted by many different leaders and applied in many different situations? Or is leadership so situational that it defies any effort to formulate a general theory of leadership?

We can find *elements* of a theory in the literature. Yet trying to piece together a comprehensive theory of leadership from the numerous threads running through the extensive literature is like trying to find one's way out of a jungle without a map.

Consider the notions of effective leadership listed in the figure on the following page. While they may prove interesting and even enlightening individually, even together, they are not a *principal path*— the essence of leadership.

A Way Out of the Jungle

What brings us out of the jungle? Is it in the leader's *ability to reason?* Is it in the leader's *sources of power?* Is it in the leader's *knowledge?* Is it in the leader's ability to carry out *core leadership functions?* Is it in the leader's *character?* Or is it in *all* of these? And to what degree does the effective leader possess these attributes?

Warren Bennis provides us with a linchpin for integrating the manifold notions about effective leadership:

> The process of becoming a leader is much the same as the process of becoming an integrated human being. For the leader, as for an integrated person, life itself is the career. Discussing the process in terms of "leaders" is merely a way of making it concrete.
>
> Warren Bennis
> *On Becoming a Leader*

3

- **Plato:** Effective leaders are *philosopher-kings*.

- **Machiavelli:** Effective leaders are *power-wielders*, individuals who employ manipulation, exploitation, and deviousness to achieve their own ends.

- **Weber:** Effective leaders have *charisma*—that special spiritual power or personal quality that gives an individual influence over large numbers of people.

- **Taylor:** Effective leaders view management as a *science*.

- **DePree:** Effective leaders view management as an *art*.

- **Drucker:** Effective leaders are able to carry out the *functions* of *management*: planning, organizing, directing, and measuring.

- **Appley:** Effective leaders have mastered the art of *getting things done through others*.

- **McGregor:** Effective leaders understand *the human side of enterprise*.

- **Likert:** Effective leaders are able to establish effective *management systems*.

- **Blake and Mouton:** Effective leaders choose a *leadership style* that reflects a concern for both production and people.

- **Iacocca:** Effective leaders focus on the three "P's": *people, product, and profit*—in that order.

- **Bradford and Cohen:** Effective leaders *develop people*.

- **Block:** Effective leaders *empower others*.

- **Kanter:** Effective leaders are *change masters*.

- **Bennis and Nanus:** Effective leaders have *vision* and are able to translate the vision into action.

- **Burns:** Effective leaders are able to *lift followers into their better selves*.

- **Deming:** Effective leaders *help others do quality work*.

Figure 1. Notions of Effective Leadership

In his remarkable insight, Bennis points us toward a path that focuses on the leader *as a person, a fully functioning person*. He has captured the essence of leadership and handed us a simple map we can use.

Adding to what Bennis said, here, then, is how we see the collective wisdom on leadership:

1. Leadership is generally defined as *influence*, the art or process of influencing people so that they will strive willingly toward the achievement of group goals. (Koontz, O'Donnell, and Weihrich)

2. This influence is brought about through an effective *personal relationship* between the leader and followers. The relationship "elevates" followers into their *better selves*. (James MacGregor Burns)

3. For a leader to be able to lift followers into their better selves, the leader must be at a *higher level of being* than that of the followers. (James MacGregor Burns)

4. By "higher level of being," we mean that the leader is *psychologically mature*. The degree to which the leader can create relationships which facilitate the growth of followers as separate persons is a measure of the psychological growth of the leader. (Carl Rogers)

5. A psychologically mature leader can best be defined as a *fully functioning person*. A fully functioning person is one who is using all of his or her faculties—and has developed them into a real unity. (Goethe)

Now we must address the obvious question: What is a fully functioning person?

The Fully Functioning Person

In presenting the idea of the "Encompassing," the renowned German philosopher, Karl Jaspers, provides us with a useful paradigm of leadership and human nature. Jaspers' view of the fully functioning person is based on concepts originated by the great philosophers over the ages and integrated by Jaspers into a comprehensive framework.

The essence of the Encompassing is articulated by an American philosopher/essayist, Ralph Waldo Emerson, whom Jaspers admired. Emerson said there is a rich world waiting out there to be *encompassed* by each human being. What part and how much of that world are to be brought within oneself is up to each individual; it does not enter automatically. Thus, each of us can either remain in one mode or move upwards, toward being a fully functioning person.

According to Jaspers, the "Encompassing" includes four modes:

- **Empirical existence**—living in the everyday world, seeking pleasure and avoiding pain

- **Consciousness at large**—acquiring objective knowledge, universally valid knowledge, that which is common to all

- **Spirit**—identifying with the leading ideas of movements, political parties, institutions, or organizations

- **Existenz**—achieving authentic selfhood.

These modes of being may be viewed as "levels of consciousness" or as "internal maps" that serve as a bridge between our subjective selves and the external world. They contain our views of reality and truth.

> We are not born with maps; we have to make them, and the making requires effort. The more effort we make to appreciate and perceive reality, the larger and more accurate our maps will be. But many do not want to make this effort. Their maps are small and sketchy, their views of the world narrow and misleading.
>
> M. Scott Peck
> *The Road Less Traveled*

If we are willing, we can create maps that will help us become fully functioning human beings. At the level of empirical existence, we will be able to create maps for coping with the everyday world. At the level of consciousness at large, we will be able to create maps of objective and universally valid knowledge. At the level of spirit, we will be able to create maps of leading ideas and beliefs with which we wish to identify. And then at the level of Existenz, we will become aware that we have the freedom to create our own maps. These maps then become the building blocks of our self-being. The building blocks are united by Reason, which is not unity but rather the will to unity.

Jaspers stresses that the fully functioning person is never completely stuck within a single mode of being. All modes are available as the fully functioning person smoothly moves between them.

The modes of being are hierarchical. Each higher level includes the lower levels, but the lower levels do not include the higher levels. And importantly, the higher levels provide direction for the lower levels. The individual in a state of *potential* Existenz resides within a lower mode of being, whereas the person who has achieved *actual* Existenz resides within the highest mode. The latter individual "lives out of the Encompassing" and is considered to be a "fully functioning person."

This, then, is the cornerstone assumption of our proposed theory of leadership: *the model leader is first and foremost a fully functioning person.* This is the person who has advanced to the mode of Existenz, while still "being at home" in the modes of spirit, consciousness at large, and empirical existence, and is guided by Reason.

The Ladder of Human Potential

Here are highlights of the importance of realizing one's potentialities:

> Birth is only one particular step in a continuum which begins with conception and ends with death. All that is between these two poles is a process of giving birth to one's potentialities, of bringing to life all that is potentially given in the two cells.
>
> Erich Fromm
> *Man for Himself*

What does it mean "to give birth to one's potentialities"? "Potential" means "capable of being or becoming." But then one asks, "Capable of being or becoming *what?*" One person has the potential for becoming an artist. Another has the potential for becoming a physician. And still another has the potential for becoming an excellent priest. There are so many possibilities!

Each individual is born with the *potential* to live out of the Encompassing—that is, to live in Jaspers' four modes. Whether or not a given individual chooses to realize this potential is a separate matter. But it's safe to assume that each individual is born with the potential to develop all of the faculties included in the Encompassing.

Fromm's second salient point is that one's main task in life is to give birth to oneself: to develop one's self as a person, a fully functioning person.

Working from within the framework of the Encompassing, we can now construct the Ladder of Human Potential, as shown below. Each rung represents an essential faculty of the fully functioning person:

- **Coping**—contending successfully with the everyday world
- **Knowing**—comprehending facts and the truth of the everyday world
- **Believing**—identifying with the leading ideas of movements, political parties, institutions, or organizations
- **Being**—achieving authentic selfhood.

Again, the four faculties are hierarchical. The higher faculties come into being only through the effects of the lower faculties, but the lower faculties are given direction by the higher faculties. The effective leader continues the venture of self-development and moves up the ladder, understanding the merits of each rung and never getting completely stuck at a given rung. With Reasoning uniting the four faculties and with all faculties intact, the leader has unlimited potential for scaling the mountain.

> Man can achieve much by using his individual faculties appropriately, he can do extraordinary things when he begins to combine them, but the supreme achievements only come when all his faculties are united. . . . Man must develop all his human capacities—his senses, his reason, his imagination, his understanding, into a real unity.
>
> Goethe
> Fairley—A *Study of Goethe*

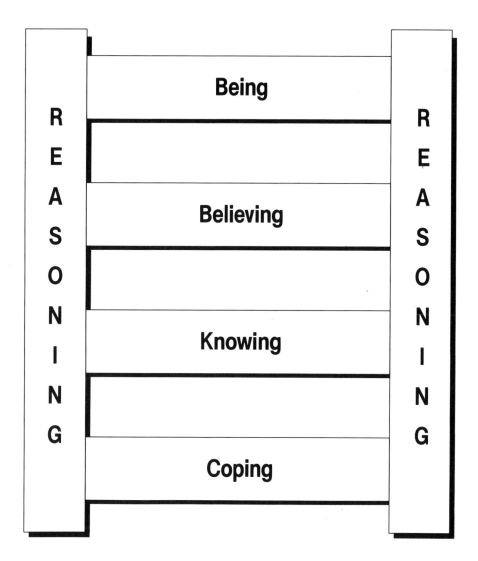

Figure 2. The Ladder of Human Potential

Putting Theory into Practice

Now we unfold the proposed theory of leadership in the form of a basic assumption and a corollary. The model leader is first and foremost a fully functioning person, and second, the fully functioning person lives out of the Ladder of Human Potential.

> Every management act rests on assumptions, generalizations, and hypotheses—this is to say, on theory. Our assumptions are frequently implicit, sometimes quite unconscious, often conflicting; nevertheless, they determine our predictions that if we do *a*, *b* will occur. Theory and practice are inseparable.
>
> Douglas McGregor
> *The Human Side of Enterprise*

The connection between the faculties in the Ladder of Human Potential and specific leadership competencies is a blend of deductive and inductive approaches. The deductive approach works from the conceptual framework provided by the concept of the Encompassing down to specific leadership competencies. The inductive approach analyzes the results of empirical studies on leadership competencies and integrates these findings in the conceptual framework provided. By combining the two approaches, we can view both the forest and the trees.

Here's how it works. The Ladder of Human Potential reveals five important human faculties—coping, knowing, believing, being, and reasoning. These faculties each translate into a corresponding dimension of leadership, which can then be subdivided into specific leadership competencies. At the practical level, the leader needs to understand these specific competencies. But the leader's understanding of the specific competencies can be enriched through a grasp of the conceptual framework.

The first translation is from "reasoning" to "reason." Reason is the sum of the intellectual abilities. The model leader possesses these five intellectual abilities: dealing with ideas and concepts, thinking logically, thinking creatively, thinking holistically, and communicating. Jaspers' definition of reason as "the total will to communication" closely connects reason and communication.

The second translation is from "coping" to "sources of power." The effective leader can cope successively with the problems and challenges of the everyday world. The leader needs power—which is simply the ability to influence others to get things done. There are three important sources of power: a staff of competent people, relevant information, and networks with others who can provide information and resources. Any leader who possesses all these resources has a tremendous amount of potential power.

The third translation is from "knowing" to "knowledge." This is straightforward: we move from a verb to a noun. There are five essential types of knowledge needed by the modern-day leader: knowing oneself, knowing the job, knowing the organization, knowing the business one is in, and knowing the world. Lacking any one of these sources of knowledge handicaps a leader.

The fourth translation, from "believing" to "core leadership functions," is more involved. For most of the present century, there has been a clear delineation of *management* functions: planning, organizing, staffing, directing, and controlling. Now, *leadership* has evolved its own core functions: valuing, visioning, coaching, empowering, team building, and promoting quality. "Believing" is the linchpin for these leadership functions.

In translating "being" to "character," we view the leader as a person with salient personality characteristics: a sense of identity, independence, authenticity, responsibility, courage, and integrity. For a given leader to be considered a fully functioning person, all six attributes are essential.

The following figure provides a list of the 25 leadership competencies. This list is not exhaustive. Certainly there are others. But the ones listed are most critical to successful leadership.

What we have here is a *tentative* theory of leadership. To evolve it into a *fully tested* theory of leadership, we must correlate the 25 leadership competencies with measures of leadership effectiveness. Nevertheless, the preliminary theory can be put to use immediately.

As you move through the following chapters, with their case studies and discussion, see how the tentative theory of the leader as a fully functioning person can apply to such immediate applications as:

• Developing leadership competencies within yourself

REASON	• Conceptual Skills • Logical Thinking • Creative Thinking • Holistic Thinking • Communication
SOURCES OF POWER	• Staff • Information • Networks
KNOWLEDGE	• Knowing Oneself • Knowing the Job • Knowing the Organization • Knowing the Business One Is In • Knowing the World
CORE LEADERSHIP FUNCTIONS	• Valuing • Visioning • Coaching • Empowering • Team Building • Promoting Quality
CHARACTER	• Identity • Independence • Authenticity • Responsibility • Courage • Integrity

Figure 3. Leadership Competencies

- Formally educating and training leaders
- Selecting individual contributors in the work place for leadership positions
- Evaluating leaders
- Educating young people at the high school level to become leaders.

Successfully using the theory for those purposes is no small accomplishment. We believe it can be done and have to agree with Kurt Lewin that "There is nothing so practical as a good theory."

Given this theoretical framework, we will now explore the five dimensions of leadership and the 25 leadership competencies.

CHAPTER

II

REASON

The philosopher's ideal is that of a rational being coexisting with other rational beings. He wants to doubt, he thirsts for objections and attacks, he strives to become capable of playing his part in the dialogue of ever-deepening communication, which is the prerequisite of all truth and without which there is no truth.

Karl Jaspers
Way to Wisdom

$\mathscr{T}$he leader who has reached the top rung of the Ladder of Human Potential—to that of Being—is guided by Reason, which connects the four modes of existence. Reason promotes unity in one's thinking. Each thinking person is bombarded with multitudinous facts and concepts, which are often diffuse and contradictory. Reason can consolidate these disparate facts and concepts into a meaningful whole.

Reason is constantly on the move. It questions, searches, tests, and answers. And the answers often are considered only tentative—to be revised as new truths are uncovered.

Reason subjects itself to criticism. Never arriving at a state of completion, Reason is constantly in the process of achieving ever-closer approximations of truth. With this in mind, persons of Reason will search out those who will challenge and disagree.

Reason assures that there is no monopoly of truth. No individual or group is the sole source of truth. Thus, truth is available to us all—regardless of our professional, political, or religious leanings.

Reason links all persons. Reason allows us to make real contact with individuals of different cultures, who may speak a different language, and who may even be our adversaries.

And finally, Reason is open to all. It is not the exclusive property of the professional philosopher. Reason is available to each person who wishes to question and to use his or her rational powers in the search for truth.

We will describe Reason in terms of these five salient abilities:

- **Conceptual Skills**—the ability to deal with high-order abstraction and generalization.

- **Logical Thinking**—the ability to apply a systematic approach in solving problems.

- **Creative Thinking**—the ability to bring imaginative ideas into being.

- **Holistic Thinking**—the ability to grasp the total situation.

- **Communication**—the ability to engage in genuine dialogue with others, to reason with others in a mutual search for truth.

Conceptual Skills

The new business leaders will be those who can stretch their minds beyond the management of physical resources. They will have the capacity to conceptualize broad new philosophies of business, and translate their vision into operation. To the traditional skills of managing people, material, machines, and money, they will add a challenging new skill—management of ideas.

Melvin Anshen
"The Management of Ideas"

18

⇒✵⇐

$\mathscr{R}$eginald was a good businessman but he didn't put much stock in ideas or concepts. As vice president for finance in a medium-sized company, Reginald was what one might consider a real pragmatist. He and I were having dinner together to discuss a business matter.

After completing the business part of the meeting, I thought it would be appropriate to switch topics. I broached the subject of a book that I had just finished reading—A World of Ideas by Bill Moyers. I pointed out that Moyers' book was a distillation of the ideas of some of our greatest thinkers. It contained transcripts of interviews that Moyers had with such notable persons as Isaac Asimov, Robert Bellah, Sissela Bok, James MacGregor Burns, Noam Chomsky, Tom Wolfe, and many others. The topics included religion, politics, law, medicine, genetics, the environment, education, poetry and literature, and on and on. Essentially, I gave Reginald a ten-minute synopsis of the stimulating ideas in the book. I knew that I was inspired by the ideas in Moyers' book, but I didn't feel that I had Reginald's full attention.

Then Reginald asked me a surprising, but perhaps revealing, question. He looked straight at me and asked, "What's the bottom line?"

Reginald may be typical of those managers whose only reality is the bottom line. Reality is found in numbers, facts, data, and financial reports. Ideas and concepts, such as those found in Moyers' beautiful book, smack of philosophy, speculation, and poetry. What do they have to do with the realities of the business world?

Unlike Reginald, who is uncomfortable in the presence of ideas, effective leaders are at home both in the world of facts and figures and in the world of ideas and concepts. Such leaders realize that ideas and concepts underlie the facts and figures.

While ideas are not as concrete or tangible as people, material resources, and money, they nevertheless are real. Ideas are the stuff out of which people, material resources, and money grow. And ideas deserve due regard by all managers.

Ideas give birth to action and products. Consider, for example, the present-day photocopying machine, a device that many would consider indispensable. It all started as an *idea* in the head of one individual.

As a law student during the Depression era, Chester Carlson could not afford to buy the textbooks required for his classes, so he spent long hours in the law library copying page after page. After numerous hours, days, and weeks of transcribing, he thought there must be a way of transferring the printed material from one page to another. And it is a fascinating story that unfolds from this idea to the Xerox machine and the Xerox Corporation. Indeed, it started out only as an idea. But what an idea!

Ideas are fragile and need nourishment. How many times you and I have seen ideas "die on the vine" before their time. Many of these ideas had great potential but something happened along the way to cause their premature death.

The work environment can either foster or inhibit the development of ideas. Certainly, an idea needs a creator, but the creator also must reside in an environment or a social milieu that will help nourish the idea to fruition. Either the creator or the environment acting alone is not sufficient. But given an individual who can generate ideas and an environment that fosters the generation of ideas, the stage is set for fruitful idea development.

An idea begins in the head of one person, but several heads are usually better than one. It is interesting and instructive to watch an idea-development discussion. One person comes up with idea A, which is then enhanced by a second person, and we now have idea A_1. Then a third person chimes in, and we now have idea A_2. And so the process continues until there is an amalgamation of ideas that may be far removed from the initial idea. The significant point is that this amalgamation probably could not have been created by any single individual acting alone.

Even though we sometimes witness an amalgamation of ideas, realize that ideas do have "owners." For example, in conducting a management seminar on the subject of motivation, I usually begin the first session with a warm-up exercise. I ask the participants, first, to list three things or events in their work experience that have *motivated* them and, second, to list three things or events that have *demotivated* them. In almost every session, someone lists as a demotivator a time when a manager *stole* his or her idea. This is sad but true. Just as homes, automobiles, and pets have owners, ideas also have owners.

Bob Maringer, a retired Battelle scientist, likens ideas to newborn babies. He presents some interesting scenarios. Suppose, for example, that you and your spouse are the parents of a newborn baby. Proudly, you take your baby to work to show it off to your manager and co-workers. You take the baby into your boss's office, and any one of several things might happen. Your boss might ignore the baby—and proceed to talk about something business-oriented, like the unit's latest production figures. Or your boss might remark that it's an ugly baby—that you could have done better. Or your boss might take the baby and say, "I'll take this one; you go out and get another one." Any of these responses would certainly be demotivating. How easy and motivating it would be for the manager to say it's a cute or healthy or strong looking child and wish you success in raising it.

As an effective leader, there are many ways to promote the development of ideas among your staff. First and foremost, you should regard management of ideas as an integral part of your job. We need to go beyond the traditional management textbook definition of a manager's job as one of making decisions regarding people, physical resources, and financial resources, to a definition of "making decisions regarding people, physical resources, financial resources, and ideas."

A manager of ideas creates an environment that fosters the generation of ideas. Quality performance and continuous improvement should be the watchword. To this end, ideas should be welcomed from everyone in your unit—from manager to staff personnel to receptionist. While you can't implement every idea that is proposed, at least you can acknowledge each idea.

Share your organization's plans with all the staff, and let them know what kinds of ideas are needed. Your people should clearly understand the unit's vision for the future as well as the present reality. The perceived discrepancy between the vision and the present reality creates a dynamic tension that should stimulate idea generation.

Support your staff as they pursue specific ideas. Treat ideas gently and nourish them, especially in their early stages of development when ideas are most susceptible to extinction. Be a sensitive leader, listen actively, and offer constructive questions that encourage a staff member to nurture a given idea.

Wait to evaluate new ideas. Yes, eventually each idea must be evaluated for its potential usefulness. But if an idea gets a negative evaluation too early in its development, a potentially fruitful idea might easily be squelched. Instead, focus on asking questions that stimulate further thinking rather than offering judgmental responses.

Most important, give appropriate recognition and due credit to individual staff members for their ideas. And if a particular idea cannot be implemented, get back to the idea's originator with a response and a reason why. Without this feedback, new ideas will "dry up."

Create an environment where ideas are viewed as "intellectual property" (which is just as valuable as other types of property). Encourage everyone in your unit to contribute to the treasure of intellectual property. By doing so, you will have achieved a great deal.

Logical Thinking

*What you might take over from the scientist—
and what the scientist might apply to problems
outside his specialty—is the habit of approaching
problems in an organized way. Problem solving
is not merely the search for order. It is the establishment and cultivation of order once it is discovered.*

Edward Hodnett
The Art of Problem Solving

⇒✳⇐

$\mathcal{A}$s a department manager in a high-tech firm, Marty gauges the department's performance on the basis of monthly time-on-projects figures. If a department can average 75 percent time-on-projects, it will usually fare pretty well in generating bottom-line profits. For the first three months of the year, Marty's department had averaged only 65 percent on this critical measure.

Being concerned about the first-quarter figures, Marty called a meeting with his five section managers to deal with the time-on-projects issue. The meeting was scheduled a week in advance and was to last for one hour.

Marty announced that it would be a problem solving meeting, but he was overly generous in describing it as such. The meeting did uncover some problems, but it did not actually solve any problems. Training specialists could have videotaped the meeting and then used the videotape as an educational film to illustrate how *not* to conduct a problem solving meeting.

Marty had just opened the meeting by attempting to define the problem when Jennifer challenged him as to whether time-on-projects was an accurate measure of the department's performance. Wasn't it true that the department's profit figures for the first three months were almost on target? After all, the department had recently completed several fixed-price contracts that had made money. So even if the time-on-projects percentages were down, what was the problem?

Before Marty could respond to Jennifer's question, Mike clearly defended Jennifer's viewpoint. He noted that the department staff had written an unusually large number of proposals during the first quarter. All of this proposal writing time had been charged to overhead and would be amortized over the year. These proposals were certain to lead to more work and the time-on-projects percentages would certainly increase over the next nine-month period.

Marty was reflecting on Mike's point when Carol proposed a solution. It was true that her section had a fairly good backlog of work in the form of signed contracts. She could accelerate the work by putting more of her staff's time on projects and reducing their time on over-head activities.

Marty acknowledged that Carol's suggestion was reasonable, but then James returned to the issue of whether or not the department actually had a problem. As long as the bottom-line profit figures were satisfactory and the department was heavily involved in marketing ac-tivities, what was the big deal about time-on-projects?

Before Marty could respond to James's question, he realized that it was 10 o'clock, the designated time for the meeting to end. He then adjourned the meeting by saying, "Well, think about the problem and we'll get back together at a later date to pursue it."

You can well imagine that this meeting was frustrating for the sec-tion managers. But they were not surprised, because Marty typically conducted all his meetings this way.

In contrast to Marty, the effective leader knows how to conduct a productive problem solving meeting. By uniting logical thinking and basic human relations skills, the effective leader can guide a group of people through a systematic problem solving process that generates a solution the entire group will accept and support.

In arranging a problem solving meeting, carefully consider the in-dividuals to be included. A good number of participants for a problem solving meeting is five or six. Each person selected should have something to contribute and/or be expected to implement the proposed solution. Consider the complementary skills: for example, one person might be selected because of his or her creative abilities while another is selected because of his or her analytical abilities.

Success in problem solving requires that the focus be on overcom-ing surmountable obstacles. It is very easy for a group to go down the road of discussing insurmountable problems and then, finally, end in dismay. But the leader's job is to refocus on those problems the group can solve.

A problem clearly defined is half-solved. Before proceeding to the solution-generation phase, be sure the problem has been clearly defin-ed. And be sure it is the *real* problem and not merely a *symptom* of the real problem.

Focusing on the wrong cause of the problem can do more harm than good. As you consider the various possible causes of the problem, be sure that you pinpoint the actual cause. A correlation between two variables does not necessarily mean that there is a cause-and-effect relationship.

The *idea-generation* phase should be separated from the *idea-evaluation* phase. After the problem has been clearly defined, it is often useful to move into a brainstorming phase in which there is one basic rule: no evaluation. Experience shows us that premature evaluation can often snuff out creative ideas. Hold off any evaluation until after all the new ideas are duly recorded and understood.

Disagreement between and among participants can be abrasive or creative—depending on the leader's skills. Anytime you assemble a group of independent thinkers for problem solving, you can expect conflict. And indeed, this conflict of ideas can generate the most fruitful ideas. So take conflict as a given. But minimize its possible negative impact by keeping the group focused on the common goal: to solve the problem.

And be aware that identifying a solution does not end the process. By writing a solution on the flipchart, some mathematically oriented individuals believe the problem is solved. Not so. What still remains is to implement the proposed solution in the real world. For this reason, you must broaden the problem solving discussion to include implementation steps—focusing on likely obstacles and how to overcome them. So remember to include those who must implement the solution in the problem solving meeting. This involvement will serve a twofold purpose: it will enhance the implementers' understanding of the problem and it will most likely enhance their motivation to work on implementing the solution.

These basic principles sound like common sense. But, as we observe managers in their problem solving efforts, we realize how few of these basic steps are commonly used.

In his book, *The Art of Problem Solving*, Edward Hodnett suggests that "What you might take over from the scientist is the habit of approaching problems in an organized way." How true! While many people actually run away from problems, scientists actively seek out problems. This is their stock in trade.

Grounded in the scientific method, a systematic approach to problem solving would go something like this:

1. Clearly define the problem.
2. Collect the facts.
3. Identify the causes of the problem.
4. List the driving forces.
5. List the restraining forces.
6. Generate alternative solutions.
7. Evaluate the alternative solutions.
8. Develop a plan of action.
9. Implement the plan of action.
10. Follow up.

This systematic approach does indeed work. It can be adapted to almost any kind of problem—financial, technical, or human. Your challenge is to master it, apply it in your own individual efforts, and employ it as a strategy in group problem solving efforts.

> Learning to solve problems is like learning to play baseball. You learn to throw, to catch, to bat, to run bases, to make plays, and to execute all sorts of refinements of these basic skills. You do not learn to play baseball. You learn these basic skills separately, and you put them together in new combinations every game.
>
> Edward Hodnett
> *The Art of Problem Solving*

Creative Thinking

Mankind is not divided into two categories, those who are creative and those who are not. There are degrees of the attribute. It is the rare individual who has it in his power to achieve the highest reaches of creativity. But quite a high proportion of the population could show some creativity some of the time in some aspect of their lives.

John Gardner
Self-Renewal

⇒✕⇐

*W*hen Staci first became manager of new product development, she informed her staff that she would welcome their creative input. But her actions have not been consistent with her words. She has not "walked the talk."

One would surely think that the success of a product development department would rest squarely on the level of creativity found among its staff. And this is what Staci told her staff when she took over as manager of the department. Initially, the staff believed that their department manager was sincere in her call for creative thinking. But during the year they became disillusioned. Their reasons for the disillusionment are easy to understand.

Consider, for example, Staci's behavior in staff meetings. At least once a month she calls a group meeting supposedly to generate new ideas. Her words and actions in these meetings, however, often inhibit creative thinking.

In one such meeting, Robin presented a novel idea only to have it quickly squelched. Staci responded to Robin's idea by asking, "Wouldn't that be a bit risky?" Robin thought to herself, "Of course, the idea would be a bit risky. Aren't *all* new ideas a bit risky?" And that was the end of Robin's active involvement in that particular meeting.

Sometimes, it is not only Staci's words that inhibit creativity, but also her body language. Whenever a staff member presents an idea that Staci doesn't fully understand or doesn't agree with, she responds very clearly through her facial expression and body posture. It is as though she might be thinking, "That's a pretty dumb idea." And whenever this happens—which is not infrequently—the active involvement of the team members is over.

Another impediment is how rarely Staci responds to individual staff members who submit new ideas via memos. Only when Staci agrees with the idea, will she get back to the person. As a consequence, some of the staff have simply stopped sending memos on new ideas.

While all of the above actions are certainly questionable, Staci has done one thing that is unpardonable—at least as far as her staff members

29

are concerned. She has stolen their ideas. On more than one occa-
sion, a department staff member has proposed a new idea to Staci and
then, several weeks later, discovered that Staci had proposed the very
same idea to her manager as though it were her own. If this happened
only once, one might forgive it as a chance occurrence or memory lapse.
But because it has happened several times, the staff have begun to question Staci's integrity.

In contrast to Staci, the effective leader creates a climate that fosters
creative thinking within the work group. This leader understands the
creative process, the factors that inhibit it, and how to promote creative
thinking.

Anyone who wants to understand the creative process should note
how Rollo May elucidates the creative process and how to enhance it.

> Creativity must be seen in the work of the scientist as well as in
> that of the artist, in the thinker as well as the aesthetician; and
> one must not rule out the extent to which it is present in captains
> of modern technology as well as in a mother's normal relation-
> ship with her child. Creativity, as *Webster's* rightly indicates, is
> basically the process of *making*, of bringing into *being*.
>
> Rollo May
> *The Courage to Create*

Given this definition of creativity, May clarifies the fundamental
aspects of the creative process and makes several major points.

The first thing in the creative act is an *encounter*. Here the individual
confronts a situation—a problem that must be solved, a need that must
be met, or a chaotic condition that is crying for order.

The source of creative production is the *struggle with limits*. If one
can move in a straight line from the present situation to the goal, there
is little call for creative thinking. But when limits are imposed—for
example, insufficient time, lack of money, or lack of known science
or technology—there is a genuine struggle. And this struggle is the
source of creative thinking.

The encounter and the struggle with limits lead to a specific *engagement*. This engagement is not limited to the intellectual domain nor
does it take place only from 8 a.m. to 5 p.m. at the place of work.

Frequently, it is a total engagement, absorbing the creator's total being and during all hours of the day—or night.

You cannot *will* to have insights, but you can *will* to give yourself to the encounter. This is perhaps one of May's most important points. You cannot simply force out creative ideas on a given day. But you can ponder the problem, be engaged in it, and struggle within its limits. Thus, it is likely that creative ideas will eventually emerge, if not to-day, perhaps tomorrow.

The subconscious mind works *to complete the incomplete Gestalt*. By "Gestalt" we mean the pattern or configuration of the desired end result. Throughout the course of engagement and the struggle with limits, your conscious mind is actively moving toward the completed Gestalt— to solve the problem—but you constantly come up against walls that seem insurmountable. Fortunately, your subconscious mind is col-laborating with your conscious mind. And, as you are taking a walk, sipping a drink, doing a routine task, or thinking about some apparently unrelated problem, lo and behold, you have a "Eureka!" experience. Your subconscious mind has served you well.

This insight often comes at a moment of *transition* between work and relaxation. Consider, for example, a certain day at work when you struggled the entire day for a creative solution to a specific problem. But regardless of your effort, nothing came forth. Then, when driving home from work that evening with the car radio playing soft music, the insight came forth. This is not a rare experience.

The breakthrough in creativity often carries with it an element of *anxiety*—because the individual is forced to seek a new foundation, the existence of which is not yet known. Individuals engaged in the creative process are well aware that they sometimes must sacrifice some peace of mind and sustain some anxiety to complete the incomplete Gestalt.

When the total engagement and the struggle with limits have finally brought about a degree of order in a perplexing situation, there is a feeling of *ecstasy*, of extreme emotional excitement. It is a beautiful feeling.

These basic principles from Rollo May's insightful book on the creative process remind us that creative thinking is not some highly mysterious or mystical experience. It is a process that can be learned. And it is a process that can be promoted and enhanced by an enlightened manager.

For those managers who desire to promote creative thinking among their staff members, these are my suggestions:

1. Be aware of the barriers to creativity, and attempt to eliminate them.

2. Create an environment in your organizational unit that fosters creative thinking—one that promotes risk-taking and is forgiving of failures when pursuing unexplored paths.

3. Develop your skills in leading group meetings designed to generate and nurture creative ideas.

4. And finally, continue to cultivate your own creative talents.

> If you do not express your own original ideas, if you do not listen to your own being, you will have betrayed yourself. Also you will have betrayed the community in failing to make your contribution to the whole.
>
> Rollo May
> *The Courage to Create*

Holistic Thinking

An essential of leadership is the ability to grasp a total situation. . . . This includes facts, present and potential, aims and purposes, and people. Out of a welter of facts, experience, desires, aims, the leader must find the unifying thread. He must see a whole, not a mere kaleidoscope of pieces. He must see the relation between all the different factors in a situation.

Mary Parker Follett
Freedom and Coordination

━━✳━━

*I*n their popular book, *The Goal,* Eliyahu Goldratt and Jeff Cox do a masterful job in pointing to the need for systems thinking. Written as a novel, this delightful book offers much practical advice for any leader who desires to achieve quality performance and continuous improvement.

The book illuminates the importance of knowing your critical success factors—the key factors that have the greatest impact on your ultimate goal. To identify these critical success factors, one must have a "systems view" of the organization.

The novel focuses on Al, a plant manager who is confronted with serious problems both at work and at home. As the general manager of a low-performing manufacturing plant, Al has been given three months to turn it around—or face the prospect of plant closure. As a genuine workaholic who frequently ignores his family, Al has been given an ultimatum by his wife, Julie, that he must spend more time with his family—or face the prospect of a dissolved marriage.

Al is indeed caught between a rock and a hard place. The situation looks almost hopeless until a chance meeting with Jonah, who was Al's college physics professor years past. Jonah is now a management consultant whose store of wisdom and experience is ideal for Al's problems at the plant. But rather than simply answer Al's specific questions, Jonah points him in the right direction through Socratic questioning. Jonah is the Greek sage personified.

Basically, Al doesn't really know how to measure progress. Without knowing what to measure, how will he know if the plant is moving forward, moving backward, or standing still? The people in the plant would have him focus on traditional measures of manufacturing efficiency. But the accountants have their own set of measures deemed important. And there is a vice president who believes that the chief measure of success is robot efficiency. In his bewilderment, Al ponders: "Where is the handle"?

Jonah, through his probing questions, gets Al to focus on the plant's primary goal and the critical factors that will have the greatest impact on whether the goal is achieved. By taking this systems approach, Al pinpoints the principal bottlenecks in the plant. Thus, he is able to restructure the entire production process to minimize the deleterious effects of the bottlenecks.

The story has a happy ending. Al saves the plant and gains a promotion. In the process, he also saves his marriage. All of this is achieved thanks to his one-time professor, Jonah, who is a systems thinker of the first order.

Why is systems thinking such a rarity? In a profound book, *The Fifth Discipline*, Peter Senge focuses on the problem: "From a very early age, we are taught to break apart problems, to fragment the world. This apparently makes complex tasks and subjects more manageable, but we pay a hidden enormous price. We can no longer see the consequences of our actions; we lose our intrinsic sense of connection to a larger whole."

Senge identifies a major problem: Many of us have been taught to analyze and understand the individual trees in the forest, but in the process, we have lost sight of the forest. To help managers move from such highly specialized thinking to systems thinking, Senge offers several important principles:

1. The essence of mastering systems thinking lies in seeing patterns where others see only events and forces to react to.
2. Systems thinking means translating a complex situation into a coherent story that illuminates the causes of problems and how they can be remedied in enduring ways.
3. Systems thinking finds its greatest benefits in helping us distinguish high-leverage from low-leverage changes in highly complex situations.
4. Nothing happens until there is vision—which stimulates movement from the *status quo*.
5. Vision without systems thinking ends up painting lovely pictures of the future with no deep understanding of the forces that must be mastered to move from here to there.

By understanding Senge's principles, managers can put systems thinking into effect—that is, holistic thinking. Here are some guidelines.

First and foremost, you must **view your organization as a system**.

Conceive of your organization as a collection of interrelated elements directed toward a common goal. Think of your organization as comprised of causal variables, intervening variables, and end-result variables. By understanding the cause-and-effect relationships, you will be better able to distinguish high-leverage and low-leverage variables.

Second, **be accurate and honest in describing the present reality of your organizational unit**. Endeavor to fully understand the present reality of your unit as a system and communicate this present reality to your staff.

Third, **work with your staff to create a vision for your organizational unit**. The vision is a clear mental picture of a desired future. It describes what you want to become. It should be challenging yet attainable.

Fourth, **foster creative tension** by holding the vision and concurrently telling the truth about current reality. Given that your staff members understand present reality and are committed to the vision, the tension between the two states of the system can promote and sustain a high degree of healthy motivation.

Fifth, to reduce the discrepancy between the present reality and the vision, **work with your staff to develop a practical strategic plan** that integrates all your key elements. This plan should be a road map for moving from the present state of the system toward the desired state.

Sixth, **continuously evaluate the progress** of your unit in the light of the vision. Are you moving toward or away from the vision? Or are you standing still? If progress is not satisfactory, what ought to be done?

Throughout this six-step strategy, the focus should be on your unit as a system . . . you and your team will thus see the trees *and* the forest. As a result, expect at least three benefits:

1. You and your staff should be able to establish priorities. By viewing the organization as a whole rather than as an assemblage of unrelated elements, you will prioritize your needs.

2. You can prevent "suboptimizing." When Al was concentrating on the measure of robot efficiency, he was indeed suboptimizing. High percentages on this measure—while perhaps satisfying to the vice president who authorized the purchase of the robots— were actually counterproductive to the plant's ultimate goal.

3. A systems approach will help you and your staff identify the high-leverage actions that are needed to achieve your goal and set the stage for a more substantial return on your efforts.

Eventually, systems thinking forms a rich language for describing a vast array of interrelationships and patterns of change. Ultimately, *it simplifies life* by helping us see the deeper patterns lying behind the events and the details.

Peter Senge
The Fifth Discipline

Communication

That people can no longer carry on authentic dialogue with one another is not only the most acute symptom of the pathology of our time, it is also that which most urgently makes a demand of us. I believe, despite all, that people in this hour can enter into dialogue, into a genuine dialogue with one another.

Martin Buber
Pointing the Way

＝❊＝

$\mathcal{I}$ have asked several hundred managers this question: "How many of you can engage in honest and open dialogue with your manager?" The positive responses equal about 60 percent. But this percentage varies considerably from organization to organization and from department to department within the same organization. In an autocratic culture, the positive response may be only 20–30 percent. But in a participative culture, the positive response may be as high as 80-90 percent.

To those who give a negative response to the first question, I pose a second question: "Why *can't* you engage in honest and open communication with your manager?" The answers are revealing. These are typical responses:

- "If I criticized my manager, it might come back to haunt me."
- "My manager is known for shooting the messenger who brings bad news."
- "My manager is too busy to have a casual discussion."
- "My manager is too wrapped up in his own problems to be interested in my problems."
- "If I revealed my true thoughts and feelings to my manager, it would make me vulnerable."
- "My manager simply does not know how to listen."

It is an unfortunate person who does not feel free to engage in an open dialogue with his or her manager. And fortunate indeed is the person who can engage in such a dialogue.

Martin Buber, in his book *I and Thou*, established dialogue as the principal theme of his broad-ranging humanistic philosophy. Buber identifies three types of interpersonal communication: monologue, technical communication, and dialogue. Monologue, of course, is one-way communication, involving sending but no receiving. Technical communication is a two-way exchange but it involves only facts and information. Dialogue, the highest form of interpersonal communication, is an honest and open exchange between two authentic persons—that is, two persons who are completely themselves in the encounter.

Dialogue and leadership go hand-in-hand. Effective leadership is based upon a foundation of trust between the leader and the team members. Trust is generated through honest and open communication. There must be honest and open communication, along with trust, for effective leadership.

> A unique relationship develops among team members who enter into dialogue regularly. They develop a deep trust. . . . They develop a richer understanding of each person's point of view. Moreover, they experience how larger understandings emerge by holding one's own point of view "gently."
>
> Peter Senge
> *The Fifth Discipline*

From the time of Socrates and Confucius up to the present age, the great teachers have applied the principles of dialogue in their own lives. Dialogue works this way:

The two partners in dialogue are engaged in a mutual search for truth. In a debate, each is attempting to defeat the other, to achieve victory over the opponent. And it is unfortunate that even casual discussions between friends frequently turn into a debate. Dialogue is radically different. Here, the goal is to collaborate with the partner in a mutual search for truth. This is a different goal as well as a different attitude.

Both participants in dialogue are "fully present." Each fully concentrates on the discussion. They are physically, mentally, and spiritually immersed in the discussion.

Both participants are active listeners. A basic requirement of dialogue is listening, and this listening is not passive; it is active. Active listening is work; it requires effort.

Both participants are spontaneous and unrehearsed. A rigid agenda can easily squelch dialogue, because the presenter tries to cover all points in a prearranged order. In dialogue, both persons are spontaneous.

Both participants avoid premature evaluation. Whenever someone first proposes an idea, it seems so natural to classify it as either "good" or "bad." But in dialogue, each party attempts to fully understand an idea—by continuing to question and explore—before evaluating the idea.

Each helps the other to clarify his or her thoughts. Rather than put the partner on the defensive in trying to justify a preliminary idea, the relationship is reciprocal. Each person becomes clearer in his or her own thinking through the aid of the partner.

Both partners keep an open mind to opposing views and are willing to alter their views as new truths are uncovered. Senge says, "Larger understandings emerge by holding one's own point of view 'gently'." This is quite different from the "I am right and you are wrong" approach. Certainly, the person in dialogue is able to take a firm stand—but only after all reasonable avenues have been explored, understood, and assimilated.

Based on these basic principles of dialogue, one might ask: "Aren't they just good common sense?" Yes. But then we ask: "If they are just common sense, why aren't they commonly applied in everyday interactions?" A good question to ponder.

By internalizing these basic principles, the effective leader can enhance interpersonal communication. One result is a genuine commitment to living a life of dialogue, and of honest and open communication with others—your manager, your team members, your peers, and your customers or clients. Such a commitment must be firm and continuous—day in and day out.

You can create a climate for dialogue in your work unit. Through your words and actions, you can convey the message that it is perfectly acceptable to speak up, to be open, and to express both thoughts and feelings. Such an environment will be liberating for those who previously have worked in an environment in which open dialogue was discouraged—or even suppressed.

You also can demonstrate to your staff another essential requirement of dialogue: the courage to confront. A certain amount of conflict is only natural. Such conflict can be either debilitating or enhancing, depending on how it is dealt with. The key here is to deal with the problem. In the long run, this approach is far superior to either suppressing the hostile feelings or ventilating the feelings to a third party. When encouraging your staff members to confront others, tell them: Attack the problem rather than the person.

Most important, be a good role model for your staff. Be a good listener, listen with understanding, be willing to express both your thoughts and your feelings, and be willing to confront.

If you do successfully create an environment that fosters dialogue, expect a number of desirable outcomes. First, dialogue should help form a genuine team—a team held together in both mind and spirit. Second, it should create an environment that is less tense, because the members will not wonder what others are actually thinking or try to second-guess the others. Third, it should create a climate of trust. And it is trust that serves as the glue for a productive work team. Without a foundation of trust, all of the other efforts to develop a productive team will fail.

Dialogue is a powerful concept and a powerful practice. You are free to choose any one of three basic modes of interpersonal communication: monologue, technical communication, or dialogue. Why not choose dialogue.

> When unity of self and others is experienced and communication reaches a heightened, personal meaning, life is being lived at a peak level. At times it seems unbelievable, almost beyond reach, but when it happens it is something of awesome beauty.
>
> Clark Moustakas
> *Loneliness and Love*

III

SOURCES OF POWER

To strive for power for power's sake means to strive for nothing. He who seizes empty power ultimately grasps at emptiness. But will to power because one needs power to realize the truth in which one believes has a constructive strength.

Martin Buber
Pointing the Way

To cope is to contend with the everyday world successfully. Anyone working toward goals—or simply trying to survive—is confronted with obstacles along the way. How effectively these obstacles are dealt with is a measure of leadership effectiveness.

Successful coping requires power. In everyday language, power is the ability to do or to act, to influence others, to get things done. Power is the ability to achieve the intended results.

Historically, the notion of power once carried a negative connotation. The desire for power was associated with evil-minded individuals. Today, however, we realize that power is essential to effective leadership.

So *why* does a leader desire power? If a particular leader seeks power only to enhance his or her own ego, or if power is an end in itself, then we should be cautious in our dealings with this leader. But if some other leader seeks power to achieve reasonable ends, then we can befriend this leader. The central issue is motive.

Assuming that the desire for power is to achieve honorable ends, then we may consider the leader's major sources of power. The effective leader has three principal sources of power:

- **Staff**—a team of persons who are ready, willing, and able.
- **Information**—knowledge required to get the job done.
- **Networks**—personal contacts with whom ideas, information, and resources can be shared.

Any leader who possesses all of these assets has a considerable amount of power. This leader will be able to overcome obstacles to achieve intended results—that is, will be able to cope.

Staff

Business has become much more competitive on a worldwide basis. The answer to that challenge is no different than it's ever been: you've got to get better and better, and if you don't, you will be left behind. The key is to get the very best people you can, and then provide them with an environment that encourages them to handle these challenges the way they see fit.

James Burke
Retired Chairman of the Board, Johnson & Johnson
(in Horton—*"What Works for Me"*)

≈⚜≈

*A*aron and Jacob have similar jobs, but very different leadership styles. Both are branch managers in the information systems division of a large bank. Aaron sees himself as a leader of technology whereas Jacob views his role as a leader of people. Let's compare these two managers and examine the implications of their different leadership styles.

Aaron manages the system design branch, which is divided into four technical groups, each headed by a technical leader. There are about 30 people in the branch.

Aaron sees himself as the technical leader of the entire branch. With a master's degree in information systems and 15 years of solid technical experience, he does indeed have in-depth knowledge of his specialty. He prides himself in being the most technically competent member of the entire branch.

Aaron spends most of each day solving technical problems. He plays a major role in planning each new project and monitoring progress until project completion. If a user of the branch's technical services has a technical problem, he or she will call Aaron rather than one of the group leaders or individual specialists. Aaron is the focal point of all technical activities in the branch.

Albeit Aaron's ability to manage the technical side of the job may be commendable, his ability to manage the people side leaves much to be desired. By and large, Aaron views his staff members as a means to an end, his own end of achieving technical excellence on every project. If staff members can contribute technically, they will be allowed to remain in the branch; if not, they will be asked to leave. People are an expendable commodity.

Aaron has a good grasp of the technical skills possessed by his staff, but he knows very little about them as persons. He simply is not interested in their needs, their values, nor their aspirations. What does that have to do with the job at hand?

Because Aaron wants to control each project, he is reluctant to delegate authority to his staff. He assigns them responsibilities but very little authority to go with the responsibilities. Authority resides exclusively with the branch manager.

Aaron's staff contains some 30 individual specialists, many of whom are quite competent technically and, somewhat surprisingly, some who are self-motivated. But they operate very much as individuals, awaiting their manager's orders, and not functioning as a team.

We now shift to Jacob, who manages the data processing branch. He also has four technical group leaders and about 30 people in his branch.

As a branch manager, Jacob sees his job as that of coach and facilitator. His principal mission is to select, develop, and retain top-notch people. Most of his day is spent coaching and helping his staff and communicating with clients. He serves as an effective bridge between the users and his staff.

When it comes to solving technical problems, Jacob doesn't actually solve the problems, but he helps his people solve problems. By posing heuristic questions, he encourages the team members to solve the problems themselves. Each of these problem solving sessions with Jacob turns out to a be a learning experience for the team member.

Jacob takes a personal interest in each team member. He knows all of his staff very well—their strengths, their limitations, their values, their needs, their aspirations. He truly knows his people.

Rather than viewing team members solely in terms of where they now are or where they have been, Jacob views each staff member in terms of potential. With the proper training and support, what might this person become? Jacob then considers it his job to help the individual staff members transform potential into reality.

Rather than the traditional carrot-and-stick approach to motivation, Jacob motivates his staff through empowerment. He provides them with the tools they need to do high quality work, helps remove obstacles, and delegates authority to go with the responsibility.

Lifelong learning is the watchword in the data processing branch. Through attending formal courses and seminars and individual study, the team members stay on the cutting edge of their technology. Jacob follows this lifelong learning path as well and thus serves as an excellent role model.

The members of this branch function as a team—30 dedicated

individuals working collaboratively to achieve a common goal. Conflict is present, but it is between ideas, not between personalities. And the conflict between ideas frequently leads to higher order ideas that are superior to what any single individual could have created alone.

What Aaron and Jacob have in common is their talent and motivation. Without a doubt, both are making a significant contribution to the information systems division.

But the two managers differ substantially in how they view their jobs. Aaron still views himself as a super technologist with 30 people serving as appendages to his technical expertise. Jacob, who was an excellent computer specialist earlier in his career, has indeed made the shift from technical specialist to manager. But better than "manager," Jacob has become a first-rate "leader-manager."

Another interesting contrast between these two managers is how they perceive their staff. Aaron, by and large, views staff as a *cost*. (Profit is the difference between revenue and cost.) Thus, anything that reduces cost—while holding revenue steady—generates more profit. Jacob, on the other hand, views his staff as an *asset*. Thus, anything that enhances and enriches this asset contributes to the company's success. These two radically different views have an enormous impact on how the two managers function.

The two approaches produce significantly different results. For example, the members of the data processing branch are at a higher level of motivation and morale than those in the system design branch. Aaron's group apparently does *just enough* to retain their jobs—no more and no less. But those in the data processing branch are *doing their very best*—day in and day out. The overall productivity of the data processing branch is greater than that of the system design branch. Jacob's unit is turning out more and better work than Aaron's unit.

Part of the reason for these differences can be found in how the two managers use power. Aaron achieves power through regulating and controlling the activities of his staff. Jacob achieves power through empowering his people. The first method is constraining; the second is enhancing.

Treat people as adults. Treat them as partners; treat them with dignity; treat them with respect. Treat *them*—not capital spending and automation—as the primary source of productivity gains. These are fundamental lessons from the excellent companies research. In other words, if you want productivity and the financial reward that goes with it, you must treat your workers as your most important asset.

Tom Peters and Robert Waterman
In Search of Excellence

Information

Confucius said, "Ah Sze, do you suppose that I merely learned a great deal and tried to remember it all?" "Yes, isn't that what you do?" "No," said Confucius, "I have a system or a central thread that runs through it all."

Lin Yutang
The Wisdom of Confucius

$\Rightarrow\mathbf{\times}\Leftarrow$

*A*s a graduate student in psychology, Herbert had an unusual way of preparing for his general examinations. On the plus side, he had a very systematic approach for collecting and organizing the information. But on the negative side, he had great difficulty in retrieving the information as needed.

Herbert had a master's degree in psychology and was working toward a Ph.D. at a Big Ten university. A major hurdle—in fact, *the* major hurdle—on the way to the Ph.D. was the five-day general examinations. This five-day marathon tests the student's comprehensive knowledge of psychology via essay questions. Most of the graduate student's efforts over a two- or three-year period are directed toward preparing for these general examinations. The course work and associated study are viewed essentially as a vehicle for preparing the student to pass the comprehensive written examinations.

Practically everything that Herbert learned in his psychology course work and his study was recorded on 3 x 5 index cards. These cards were then placed in five long index card boxes, with one box for each of the five areas to be covered in the general examinations. The cards in each box were arranged in alphabetical order.

Other graduate students looked at Herbert in amazement and perhaps envy. Their colleague was indeed a store of information, or at least his index card boxes were a store of information.

Herbert's fellow graduate students who also were preparing for the general exams frequently would go to him with specific questions. Given a question, for example, about William James, Herbert would go to the box labeled "General Psychology" and look under the letter "J." Given a question about retroactive inhibition, he would go to the box labeled "Learning Theory" and look under the letter "R." And asked for a definition of homoscedasticity, he would turn to the box "Research Methodology and Statistics" and look under the letter "H."

Watching Herbert retrieve answers to these multifarious questions was indeed a novel experience. It was like watching a human computer in action.

Then came the general examinations. One would think that Herbert—the human computer—would be the best prepared of all the graduate students taking the exams. Not so.

Without the index card boxes at hand, Herbert was overwhelmed by the essay questions. On the first day of the exams, he was asked to compare and contrast the learning theories of Tolman, Skinner, and Rotter. On the second day he was asked to design an experiment to test for the effects of retroactive inhibition. Then on the third day he was asked to summarize three major personality theories, select the one he prefers, and justify his choice. And so it went for five days.

Even with all of his diligent recording and classifying, Herbert was ill-prepared for the general examinations. He simply had not organized the information in a way that would serve him well under the given test conditions. His problem was that he had not converted data and information into knowledge. One might say that he had an "overload" of data and bits of unrelated information but an "underload" of knowledge.

As expected, Herbert failed the general examinations. And sadly, he also failed them in two subsequent attempts. He then left the university, blocked by the major hurdle on the way to a Ph.D.

Herbert's problem was one of proper organizing, retrieving, and ultimately translating information into knowledge. Yet Herbert's plight was not unique; it is faced by large numbers of modern-day managers.

Effective leaders have the information needed to get the job done. They know how to collect information, how to store it, and how to retrieve it as needed. Most important, they know *what* information to collect and store.

In his book, *Management*, Peter Drucker stresses that "Managers should ask themselves: 'What information do I need to do my job and where do I get it?' They should make sure that whoever has to provide that information understands the manager's needs—not only in terms of what is needed but also how it is needed."

Good information is the essential tool for every manager. Without it, how can the manager make good decisions? And without good decisions, how can the manager be a good manager?

Information is a source of power for every manager. The key, however, is to get the *right* information at the *right* time and in the *right* form. As in Herbert's case, information by itself is insufficient. It must be selected, organized, *and* translated into usable knowledge— that is critical.

Also important is that the changing relationship between the amount of information given to the manager and the manager's performance is curvilinear. That is, the relationship is positive up to a point, it levels off, and then becomes negative. Thus, rather than *maximize* the amount of information given to the manager, we should *optimize* it.

The key to obtaining relevant information is to identify your critical success factors—areas in which satisfactory results will ensure successful performance. For a manufacturing department, the critical success factors might be quality, quantity of production, meeting schedules, equipment down time, and operating within budget. For a marketing and sales department, the critical success factors might be total sales, number of new customers, number of calls on customers, market share, and costs. And so on for other departments.

Identify your critical success factors for the next three-year time period as well as for the coming year. These sets of factors undoubtedly will be related but not necessarily identical.

To identify your critical success factors, you must understand your unit's role in the overall scheme of things and how your unit contributes to the success of the larger organization. What is the "value added" of your unit? Your answer should help formulate a clear unit mission that contributes to the mission of the larger organization.

But the unit mission is key to the unit's critical success factors. So what limited number of areas (no more than five to seven) must have satisfactory results to assure successful performance in achieving the mission?

Obviously, you must agree with your manager and your team members on your unit's critical success factors. The team members will then have a framework for establishing priorities for their own activities.

Once the critical success factors are identified and agreed upon, you can decide what accurate and timely information you need on each of these factors. This information will enable you to gauge the progress of your unit and make effective diagnostic decisions.

To collect information on the critical success factors, use a twofold approach: formal reports and personal observation. These formal reports represent "maps"; personal observation represents "territory." Tom Peters says personal observation means managing by walking around. MBWA should be employed both inside and outside the organization. That is, to find out what is going on, listen to both your people and your customers.

In other words, you must *focus*. You conceivably could collect information on several hundred factors, but then you might suffer the fate of Herbert, the psychology graduate student. You do not need information on several hundred factors. Instead, get accurate and timely information on only a select few factors—your critical success factors. Focus on them.

> The binding fact of mental life is that there is a limited capacity for processing information—our span, as it is called, can comprise six or seven unrelated items simultaneously. Go beyond that and there is overload, confusion, forgetting. As George Miller has put it, the principle of economy is to fill our seven mental-input slots with gold rather than dross. The degree to which material to be learned is put into structures by the learner will determine whether he is working with gold or dross.
>
> Jerome Bruner
> *On Knowing*

Networks

The failure of hierarchies to solve human problems has forced people to begin talking with one another outside their organizations, and that is the first step to forming a network. Clusters of people have come together to communicate about, and attempt to address, the concerns and problems that traditional structures have failed to address.

John Naisbitt
Megatrends

⇒✴⇐

C harles and Nancy are training directors in two different companies in the same city. What they have in common is that they are both highly competent and highly motivated training specialists. How they differ is that one has a network and one does not. Their principal differences are illustrative to both training directors and all managers.

Charles is the training director for a medium-size manufacturing firm. He reports to the director of human resources and has three training specialists and one secretary reporting to him. His unit designs, conducts, and evaluates all the company's training.

Before entering the private sector, Charles served eight years as an officer in the U.S. Air Force. This tour of duty allowed him to get a master's degree in instructional technology and gain considerable practical experience in instructional design. He also had a substantial opportunity to learn about chain of command.

Charles is highly competent in instructional development. He has mastered the tools and techniques of job analysis, needs assessment, instructional design, media selection, and program evaluation. Through a combination of academic work and practical experience he has learned how to put theory into practice.

Charles and his team members have a fairly standard approach for developing a new training program. First, the request comes from the director of human resources. What then follows is a review of the relevant literature, a collection of material, a preliminary design of the course, and a pilot test of the program. After making appropriate revisions, the program is offered to a target group in the company.

Charles and his staff used such a systematic strategy in developing a Total Quality Management training program intended for all company managers. The impetus for this particular training came from the company's CEO, who had established TQM as the company's number one priority. The TQM seminar was to be an integral part of the company's TQM program. Charles and his team did develop a sound management seminar—but it took 18 months. This lengthy development cycle annoyed the CEO, whose call to the director of human resources prompted a great deal of explaining and apologizing.

Charles's basic problem is that he has no network beyond four staff members and his manager. Outside of these five individuals, he has very few contacts.

On a typical day, Charles spends most of his time in his office, working diligently on one or more training projects. He spends a small amount of time interacting with his team members and perhaps once a week meets with his manager to review progress. During the lunch hour, Charles usually eats alone in his office and reads a professional journal.

Inside the company, Charles operates as a good worker. Before initiating any significant action, he seeks his manager's approval. The traditional chain of command is the only paradigm that Charles understands.

Given this brief description of how Charles carries out his responsibilities as training director, we now switch to the other side of the city. Here we find Charles's counterpart, Nancy, the training director for a medium-size service organization. Nancy also reports to the director of human resources. She has two training specialists and an administrative assistant reporting to her. She and her staff design, conduct, and evaluate all training in the company.

Her strength lies in her ability to network with others. Even in high school and college, Nancy had a knack for networking with other people. And she has carried this special talent to her present job as training director. It has paid great dividends.

Nancy has numerous close contacts within the company, and knows practically everyone else by name. Whenever she is not meeting with someone on the outside, she eats lunch in the company cafeteria. She makes a point of sitting with different groups of people each day.

These casual discussions are invaluable to her as she learns about employee concerns and especially about their training needs.

On a somewhat more formal basis, Nancy frequently tours the organization talking with her clients—the line managers of the company. These frequent contacts help Nancy grasp her clients' training needs. She also seeks feedback on how well her unit is meeting those needs.

Outside the organization, Nancy plays an active role in professional associations. She is an officer in both the American Society of Training

Directors and the local Personnel Managers Association. She also participated in the Area Leadership Program. These affiliations have given Nancy numerous outside contacts, both locally and nationally.

This networking manager has more than 100 personal contacts in the field of training. These are the individuals she keeps in contact with on a continuing basis. Whenever she is searching for specific information, she usually can get it by making one or two telephone calls. And she has a reputation for being a provider of useful information.

When the director of human resources asked Nancy to develop a management seminar in Total Quality Management, she did it in a record time of three months. By contacting individuals in her network, she was able to collect an abundance of materials in less than one month. She and her staff then organized the program in the second month and pilot tested it in the third month. The response of the participants in the pilot program was outstanding. When word reached the CEO, he made a special point of expressing his appreciation to the director of human resources, to Nancy, and to her staff.

When the CEO was meeting with Nancy and her staff to commend them on their excellent work, he mentioned that the next step in the Total Quality Management program was to begin benchmarking against other organizations. Nancy was able to again tap into her network and provide him with a list of some 20 companies and names of individuals who would be willing to share information that could be used in the benchmarking process.

Another outcome of this activity was that Nancy established a network of training directors who were especially interested in Total Quality Management. As the informal leader of this 25-member group, Nancy calls a monthly meeting in which the members share what they are doing in the area of Total Quality. This is truly a win-win endeavor.

I don't want to make it sound as though Nancy operates like a loose cannon. She doesn't. But she is a proactive person who takes the initiative, uses common sense, and gets things done. Nancy knows how the system operates and how to get things done within the constraints of the system. She knows when she should check with her manager and when to work independently. But she always keeps her manager informed of her unit's activities.

Having looked at how Charles and Nancy work, the key difference is that Nancy has a network and Charles does not. With respect to these different work styles, we can conclude:

- Nancy understands her company much better than Charles does his.
- Nancy excels Charles in understanding the training needs within the company.
- In gaining acceptance and support of new training programs throughout the organization, Nancy definitely has the edge.
- In getting things done effectively and efficiently within the organization, Nancy again has the edge.
- In staying abreast of what is going on in the field of training, Nancy is years ahead of Charles.
- In this case, Nancy's team can develop a new training program in about one sixth the time required for Charles' team.

What really accounts for these significant differences is the knowledge base. For Charles, the primary knowledge base is found in the hierarchical structure of the formal organization. The principal way he acquires information is to work through his manager. But for Nancy, the primary knowledge base is found in the network. The nurturing of these contacts both within and outside the organization is her key to success.

The lesson here is: Develop your network. Be aware of the requirements of the vertical organizational structure, but be diligent in complementing the vertical structure with lateral and diagonal linkages.

> In the network environment, rewards come by empowering others, not by climbing over them. The vertical to horizontal power shift that networks bring about will be enormously liberating for individuals. Hierarchies promote moving up and getting ahead, producing stress, tension, and anxiety. Networking empowers the individual, and people in networks tend to nurture one another.
>
> John Naisbitt
> *Megatrends*

IV

KNOWLEDGE

We live in an age of affluence in many respects. The mass media bombard us with stimuli and we have to protect ourselves by filtering them, as it were. We are offered a lot of possibilities and have to make choices among them. In short, we have to make decisions as to what is essential and what is not.

Viktor Frankl
The Will to Meaning

*M*ost leaders agree that, to be effective in their jobs, leaders need knowledge. But *what kind of knowledge* makes a leader effective?

Today we hear much about the knowledge explosion and the accelerating rate at which knowledge is being generated. Any leader knows that it is futile to try to deal with this knowledge explosion by storing in memory ever larger amounts of information. There would be no time for productive leadership.

Instead, effective leaders deal with information overload: they know how *to identify the essential.* They have a knack for separating the wheat from the chaff. They are able to skim large amounts of information and extract the essential. They then store in memory only what is essential—and they know how to store the information for easy retrieval.

Consider the question posed to a professional bridge player by an amateur player:

> *Amateur:* "How are you professionals able to store such large amounts of information during the course of play?"
>
> *Professional:* "No, that's not the case. We don't store any more information than the amateurs, but we *know* what information to store."

And so it is with professional leaders. They know *what* information to store. The model leader has five salient types of knowledge:

- **Knowing Oneself**—having a good grasp of one's own strengths and weaknesses and actively seeking feedback for the purpose of personal growth.
- **Knowing the Job**—understanding the requirements of the job and how the job contributes to the organization's goals.
- **Knowing the Organization**—understanding the culture of the organization and how to get things done effectively and efficiently.
- **Knowing the Business One Is In**—understanding the external environment sufficiently well to know the needs of clients and what represents "value" to the clients.

- **Knowing the World**—understanding the world community and how the smaller communities relate to the larger community.

Staying up to date on all five of these domains of knowledge is no small order, but the effective leader is able to do it.

Knowing Oneself

"Know thyself" was the inscription over the Oracle at Delphi. And it is still the most difficult task any of us faces. But until you truly know yourself, strengths and weaknesses, know what you want to do and why you want to do it, you cannot succeed in any but the most superficial sense of the word.

Warren Bennis
On Becoming a Leader

➤✳︎⬅︎

$\mathcal{R}$ichard and Barbara are department managers in a medium-size computer software company. Both aspire to become vice presidents in the company. One will make it and one will not.

The two department managers have a great deal in common. Both have master's degrees in computer science. Both have approximately ten years' experience with the company and three years' experience as managers. Both have a reasonably good understanding of the computer business. And both are intelligent and highly motivated managers. But here the similarity ends.

Where they differ is in how well they know themselves. Barbara has a good grasp of both her strengths and her weaknesses, whereas Richard knows his strengths but not his weaknesses. This difference will prove to be a key predictor of which one will be promoted to vice president.

When these two department managers make oral presentations to upper management, the differences in style are obvious. Richard comes across as a person who is extremely self-confident and absolutely sure that he is on the right track. Before the meeting, he rehearses two or three times. He anticipates all the likely questions and formulates an answer to each. Barbara, on the other hand, comes across as somewhat tentative in her views. She also prepares herself for the meeting. But after listening carefully to each question and reflecting on it, she will sometimes alter her views on a particular issue.

On the surface, Richard may seem the more confident—and competent—of the two. But when we penetrate the surface, this initial judgment might be wrong.

Look, for example, at these two managers leading meetings with their team members. Again, Richard comes across as a very self-confident leader who knows he is on the correct course. But these are usually one-way meetings, with Richard doing about 90 percent of the talking. When he completes the presentation, he then answers any questions the team members might raise. Barbara's approach is quite different. She gets a problem or an issue out on the table and the group discusses it. Various points of view are aired and, interestingly, the team members are not reluctant to point out weaknesses or flaws in their manager's thinking—and she listens. Sometimes the group makes the final decision on the issue and sometimes Barbara makes the final decision. In either case, once the decision is made, the entire team will support it.

These same differences show up whenever these two managers interact with others on a one-to-one basis. Richard comes across as a self-confident person who is certain of his particular stance or position on any issue. And he is unrelenting in his efforts to get the other person to "see the light." But Barbara's interactions with other individuals are more open. They often take the form of a joint exploration or a mutual search for truth.

In all these examples, a principal difference between the two managers is in their ability and willingness to listen, to *really listen*. Richard only partially listens, as he selects the specific points that he wants to rebut. But Barbara truly listens—be it in a meeting with upper management, a meeting with her team members, or a one-on-one exchange. She actively listens to whatever is said to her and shows the other person that she understands what has been said. Through this unusual ability to listen actively and understand, Barbara gains the respect of others.

One reason why Richard and Barbara have such different leadership styles is the managers for whom they have worked. Richard's managers gave him only positive feedback—never mentioning his flaws. Granted, he always has been a hard-driving, achievement-oriented manager, but this was no reason to allow his weaknesses to be ignored. Barbara, on the other hand, had two successive managers who took staff development and coaching seriously. These managers personally helped people like Barbara grow and develop. And they knew that this could be done only through honest and open discussions with their junior managers—in which both strengths and weaknesses were discussed frankly and constructively.

Greater understanding of Richard and Barbara comes from looking at them years ago. Richard grew up under a father who was a binary thinker, an individual who was convinced there was a right and a wrong to every issue—a man who was convinced that he was always right. And by shaping his two sons into this way of thinking, he created clones.

Barbara, however, grew up in a fundamentally different home environment. She remembers the open and lively discussions at the dinner table with her parents and brother. Any idea or issue could be put forth for debate and discussion. And everyone listened actively to whoever was speaking. These lively discussions frequently would bring about changes in points of view. The various positions were held "gently" and one could witness true "family learning" occurring. These dinner-table discussions profoundly influenced Barbara's personal development.

As a consequence of these differentiating experiences—from childhood up to the present day—the two managers have dissimilar self-concepts. Richard sees himself as a person who is confident and competent, who knows the answers. This is what he wants to project to others. Barbara's self concept is that of a person who is continuously learning and growing, who is striving and seeking. She views learning as a lifelong process, and she knows that she will never completely "arrive" but she will enjoy the journey. She doesn't give much thought to how she projects herself to others; she is simply herself.

"Know thyself" was the inscription over the Oracle at Delphi centuries ago. Today, this inscription still serves as sound advice for anyone who aspires to be an effective leader. To know oneself is the most difficult task any leader will face. The better you know yourself, the better your potential for being an effective leader.

In the leadership development process, this is the chain of causal relationships:

1. Self-examination is essential for self-understanding.
2. Self-understanding is essential for personal growth.
3. Personal growth is essential for leadership development.

This homily carries a single message: Decide that the only way you will ever grow is to truly know your strengths and weaknesses. And further, the only way that you will ever know your strengths and weaknesses is to solicit feedback from others.

One way to do this is to identify and recruit four or five acquaintances who will give you honest feedback on your behavior and performance. These are individuals who will be totally honest with you. These acquaintances might be peers, people who report directly to you, your own manager, your spouse, a personal friend. There is one criterion for selection: Any person selected will be *completely honest* in giving you feedback. If anyone continuously gives you only praise and positive feedback, replace this person with someone else. Surround yourself with this group of individuals who will give you feedback—good and not so good. This could be the most important thing that you will ever do in advancing your own learning.

> After you get over the pain, eventually self-knowledge is a very nice thing. It feels good to know about something rather than to wonder about it, to speculate about it.
>
> Abraham Maslow
> "Synanon and Eupsychia"

Knowing the Job

When asked what they do for a living, most people describe the tasks they perform every day, not the purpose of the greater enterprise in which they take part. Most see themselves within a "system" over which they have little or no influence. They "do their job," put in their time, and try to cope with the forces outside of their control. Consequently, they tend to see their responsibilities as limited to the boundaries of their position.

Peter Senge
The Fifth Discipline

➤✻◄

*I*n spending the better part of two weeks in two different hotels, I witnessed quality service at its best and at its worst. The staff in the first hotel knew their jobs; those in the second did not.

Assume that one is evaluating the quality of service provided by hotels on a 10-point scale, with "10" being high and "1" being low. I want to tell you about two hotels that represent the two ends of the spectrum. The first, which I will call "Hotel A," is located in a suburb of Denver. The second, which I will designate as "Hotel B," is located in the Northwest.

From the time that I checked into Hotel A until the time I checked out, I was truly impressed with the quality of service provided by the hotel staff. A friendly desk clerk had my registration card already completed with name and address, knew exactly where my seminar materials were located, and willingly and graciously answered all my questions. I found the seminar room was arranged exactly the way that I had requested. And throughout the three days, the catering service for lunches and refreshment breaks was outstanding.

But what was most appreciated was whenever I asked any staff member to do something for me, the immediate response was "You've got it." And to my delight, I always "got it." Even though the person I spoke to might not personally carry out the request, she or he would make certain it got done. The staff at the hotel made this three-day experience a pure delight.

Just before my departure, I personally thanked the hotel manager for the quality service provided by all of the staff. I mentioned to him that I was especially impressed with how every staff member responded to any request that I made—even though the request might fall outside a given staff member's job responsibilities. He then told me about the hotel's training program for all new employees. This program stresses the concept of "one-stop shopping": Whatever a customer requests of you, see that it gets done. What a sound principle! This is why I return to this particular hotel. I also should mention the large sign posted over the employee entrance to the hotel: "Quality starts here."

Now for the bad news. The "problem" of going to Hotel B after having been at Hotel A was the exceptionally high standard of excellence I had come to expect. When compared to Hotel A, Hotel B would be only a "1" or a "2" on our 10-point scale. See if you agree.

When I arrived at the airport in the city where Hotel B is located, I called the hotel to request transportation service. The hotel is less than one mile from the airport, yet some 20 to 25 minutes after my call I was still waiting at the airport. I made a second call. The operator assured me that she had announced on the intercom that Carlos should go to the airport to pick me up. Carlos, of course, did not receive the message. I then realized that the operator saw her job as that of making the announcement, not that of making certain that Carlos actually left the hotel to go to the airport and pick me up.

When I finally arrived at the reception desk, I filled out the entire registration card with name and address even though this information had been sent to the hotel previously. When I asked the desk clerk about the seminar materials that we had mailed to the hotel, she quickly pointed out that she had nothing to do with seminar materials. I would have to talk with the people in banquets. But since this was Sunday evening, no one from banquets was on duty. I simply would have to wait until Monday morning—the first day of the seminar—to find out if the materials had arrived. (Fortunately for me, early Monday morning, after an extensive search, I was able to locate the seminar materials.)

On the first morning of the seminar, I wanted to make sure that the soft drinks would be brought into the seminar room for the 2 o'clock break. I went through the rear exit of the room into the kitchen where I found several employees sitting at a table taking a break. When I mentioned that I would like to have the soft drinks brought in at 2 o'clock, one of the employees looked up at me and responded, "That's not our department."

Then on the second day of the seminar, I wanted to request a different arrangement of the chairs in the room in which we were served lunch. On the first day, the room had been set for 32 people—eight at each of four tables. Since we had only 23 participants plus me, I wanted them to set for six people at each of four tables. I found an employee who was setting up the room next to the one in which we would be served lunch. When I asked him if he would reduce the number of chairs from 32 to 24 in our room, he responded, "That's not my room for set-up; *this* is my room."

71

On the third day of the seminar, the bulb in the overhead projector went out and there was no backup bulb in or around the projector. Because I use many overhead transparencies, I needed a replacement bulb immediately. I went out into the hallway and approached the first employee I saw. After I had explained to him the urgency of my obtaining a projector bulb, he responded: "You will have to find Charlie." Can you imagine: "Find Charlie??" Here I was in a crunch, and I didn't have the slightest idea who Charlie was or where to find him.

Throughout the three-day stay, I was unable to get a morning newspaper that I could read as I ate my breakfast. I usually would go down to breakfast at about 6:30 every morning, but the gift shop—which was the only place where a newspaper could be purchased—did not open until 8:00. During a break on the third morning, I went into the gift shop to discuss the newspaper issue. I explained to the clerk that business people such as myself who travel a great deal would appreciate being able to get a newspaper at 6:30 or 7:00 in the morning. Her response was classic: "I open the gift shop at 8 o'clock every morning. Coming in any earlier than that would not be convenient for me."

And so it went for the entire three days. What bothered me most about my interactions with the staff at the second hotel was the prevailing attitude and response, "That's not my job." Each employee had a narrow, clearly prescribed set of duties, and any customer request that did not fall squarely in the domain of the employee's job description was simply of no concern to the employee.

Comparing the staff of Hotel A and the staff of Hotel B brought to mind some ideas credited to Dr. W. Edwards Deming, the world-renowned quality expert. Dr. Deming claimed that 85 percent of all performance problems trace back to management. At the time, I thought Dr. Deming was putting too much of the onus on management. But now, after my experience at Hotel A and Hotel B, I think that Dr. Deming was correct.

Why is the behavior of the staff at Hotel B so radically different from that of the staff at Hotel A? Is there a difference in level of intelligence? Probably not. Is there a different amount of formal education? Probably not. Indeed, there probably are no significant differences on any of these factors.

I agree with Dr. Deming: The problem can be traced back to

management. In Hotel B, it appears that the employees have never been told by management that their primary job is to serve customers. Nor have they been told about the importance of quality service—and that quality is defined as meeting or exceeding customer expectations. Simply put, these employees have not been properly trained for their jobs.

After presenting my complaints to the manager of Hotel B, I now wonder if he ever brought about any changes in quality of service. But I will never know—because I will never return to that hotel.

"The effective executive focuses on contribution," notes Peter Drucker in *The Effective Executive*. "He looks up from his work and outward toward goals. He asks: 'What can I contribute that will significantly affect the performance and the results of the institution I serve?'"

I would broaden Drucker's statement to include all staff. Effective staff members—managers and employees alike—should focus on contribution. They should look beyond their work and outward toward goals. Each should ask: "What can I contribute that will help meet or even exceed customer expectations?" Contributions should go beyond job descriptions.

So it's no wonder that many managers have ambivalent feelings about the utility of written job descriptions. And rightly so. While all staff should have a clear understanding of their jobs, written job descriptions tend to put people in pigeonholes. As Peter Senge puts it: "They tend to see their responsibilities as limited to the boundaries of the position."

Whether or not your organization has written job descriptions, your staff members do need to know what is expected of them:

- Define each job in terms of *contribution to the larger enterprise*.
- Show how each job *adds value* to the total organization.
- Focus specifically on how the job *helps meet customer needs*.

When jobs are described in this manner—with proper orientation and training—the staff will begin to view their jobs in terms of contributing to the mission of the enterprise. And rather than respond to a customer, "That's not my job," they will be more likely to say, "You've got it."

Knowing the Organization

It is important for all managers — or employees for that matter — to have a good and precise sense of the culture of their companies. Once you know more exactly the type of culture that you're dealing with, you will have a better idea of how to get things done in an effective way.

Terrence Deal and Allan Kennedy
Corporate Cultures

➤✹◄

$\mathcal{C}$arol and Carl were brought in from the outside to head up two different departments in an advanced energy laboratory. They both failed. And they failed for the same reason: They didn't understand the corporate culture.

The advanced energy research laboratory has a culture typical of most government-sponsored research laboratories. It was established some 10 years ago to develop alternative energy sources for U.S. industry and the American public. Technical areas of focus include nuclear, solar, fossil fuels, wind, and other potential sources of energy. The type of work done covers the gamut from basic research to applied research to development to technology transfer. With a solid reputation for quality work both in the U.S. and abroad, the laboratory has a bright future.

Practically all 2,000 employees in the laboratory have come to understand its culture—best described as a blend of freedom and control. Or even better, it is a *balance* of freedom and control. Freedom fosters creativity and innovation. Control assures that all environmental safety and health factors fully meet the compliance requirements of the sponsoring government agency.

One of the laboratory director's principal challenges is to create and maintain the conditions that assure a balance of freedom and control. Should freedom override control, the laboratory would soon be out of business—because the federal agency would not renew its contract. On the other hand, should control override freedom, the laboratory would be out of business—because creative scientists would leave.

The corporate culture can be described via the Chinese Yin and Yang. These two terms represent mutually opposing forces, with each alternating as either dominant or recessive. To the Chinese, a complete philosophy of life calls for balancing Yin and Yang.

Carol and Carl began their new jobs as department managers without understanding the opposing forces of the laboratory. One failed because of Yin, the other because of Yang. Let me explain.

Carol was brought in to head up the solar energy department comprised of some 100 scientists, engineers, and support staff. Their goal is to demonstrate the feasibility of solar energy as a viable energy source for the 21st century. The new department manager came from a university where she had gained an international reputation as a leading authority on solar energy. With 10 years' research experience and numerous publications, she was heartily welcomed to serve as the department's technical leader. She accepted the position with the understanding that she would be able to delegate many of her administrative duties, thus allowing more time for the technical leader's role.

During the interview process, which was spread over several weeks, Carol spent a total of some 24 hours in the laboratory. She met the director, the deputy directors, the department managers, and all of the group leaders in the solar energy department. Further, she got to know many researchers in the solar energy department and what they do.

Thus, Carol believed that she clearly understood the operation and its future. She liked what she saw and she accepted the job offer.

What caused Carol's failure was that she brought the university culture with her—a professional culture that fostered freedom and innovation. That was the environment in which she thrived, and it was only natural that she would expect her new employer to provide the same—or at least a similar—environment.

That was the Yin side of the equation. But she was blindsided by the Yang side.

The federal sponsoring agency had announced to the laboratory director that a team would visit the laboratory in approximately three months to conduct a complete audit of the laboratory's environmental safety and health (ES&H) program. To prepare for the audit, the director established a special team—laboratory staff who would conduct a self-assessment of the laboratory's ES&H program. After the self-assessment was completed, each department manager received a detailed report pinpointing corrective measures that must be taken before the government-sponsored team's visit.

Not fully appreciating the importance of that report, Carol simply did not give it high priority. As you might expect, the solar energy department received low marks from the formal audit. And consequently, the entire laboratory received a rating of only "Good" rather than "Excellent." One month later, Carol was no longer employed by the laboratory.

Turning now to Carl, we find a similar, yet different, situation. Carl was in the Yang mode and was blindsided by Yin.

Carl was brought into the laboratory to head up the quality assurance department. With the laboratory's mission being to carry out *quality work* in advanced energy, the quality assurance department was viewed as one of the most important units in the entire laboratory.

Carl came from a manufacturing company where he had been successful in establishing a Total Quality Management program. With more than 15 years of experience in the area of quality control, he was a recognized expert. Because of his leadership role in the national quality control professional association, his reputation preceded him. And this was how the advanced energy laboratory had come in contact with him.

Just as Carol had done, Carl spent three full days in the laboratory during the interview process. In this period of time, Carl met most of the managers and became familiar with the overall operation. He believed that the move from the world of manufacturing to the world of research and development would offer new challenges for him, so he accepted the job offer.

But Carl failed because he brought the manufacturing culture with him. All that he had known previously was a top-down culture in which orders came from "on high" and were enforced all the way down the organization. And this is how Carl assumed he would function in his new position.

During Carl's initial visits to the laboratory, he had become familiar with the compliance requirements of the government sponsor, and he saw his job as enforcing these requirements. But he went about it all wrong.

The first month on the job was exasperating for Carl. His frustration was triggered by three specific events. First, he announced by memo to all department managers a meeting to discuss Total Quality Management (TQM). At least half the managers didn't attend the meeting . . . because they didn't like the "tone" of the memo. Next, he scheduled a one-day seminar on TQM for project managers. Some project managers were present for the morning session, but most did not return for the afternoon session . . . because they thought Carl's approach to quality improvement was too "top-down." Then a week later, he met with the deputy directors to propose a method for assuring better quality control. Since written reports were the laboratory's principal product, Carl thought that all reports should be reviewed by his office before final submission to the customer. Carl presented his idea to the deputy directors . . . and they laughed.

Then, in a state of frustration, Carl went to meet with the laboratory director. As he explained his difficulties in gaining support from the other managers for his quality control program, the director listened attentively. After Carl had finished venting his frustrations, the director then proceeded to explain in some depth the laboratory's culture. He stressed that, even though it was a top-down organization when it came to complying with government requirements, it was very much a bottom-up organization when it came to gaining acceptance of new ideas and programs. In other words, it was simultaneously a top-down and a bottom-up organization. It was both Yin and Yang.

Carl was confused by this talk about Yin and Yang. To him, things were either A or non-A; they could not be both. The laboratory either was going to enforce quality control or it wasn't. It had to do one or the other.

During the next several weeks, the director held several follow-up meetings with Carl to try to explain the laboratory's corporate culture and to suggest ways by which Carl might gain acceptance from the other managers. But it never "took." Within a few months, Carl had submitted his resignation and returned to the world of manufacturing.

So here we have two highly touted managers who failed in their respective positions. Was the failure due to lack of technical competence? Not really. Was it for lack of intelligence? No. Was it for lack of motivation and dedication? Not really. Was it for lack of understanding the formal organizational structure? No. Was it for lack of understanding the laboratory's corporate culture? Yes.

And who is to blame for the failure of these two technically competent managers? The laboratory director for not fully explaining the laboratory culture to Carol and Carl during the initial interviews? Or Carol and Carl for not exploring the corporate culture in greater depth during the time of the interviews? Or perhaps both?

Here I agree with Nietzsche's advice: "Distrust all in whom the impulse to punish is powerful!" Our purpose here is not to punish but to learn from past mistakes.

The lesson here is that all members of a given organization need to understand its corporate culture. They need to understand "how we do things around here" so they can get things done effectively and efficiently. This understanding includes the nuances, the subtleties, the stuff of reality.

As a leader-manager, you must fully explain the corporate culture to both your present and your potential staff members. This may indeed be one of your most important responsibilities.

Knowing the Business One Is In

That business purpose and business mission are so rarely given adequate thought is perhaps the most important single cause of business frustration and business failure. Conversely, in outstanding businesses ... success always rests to a large extent on raising the question, "What is our business?" clearly and deliberatively, and on answering it thoughtfully and deliberatively.

Peter Drucker
Management

※

$\mathscr{D}$r. Francis Atkinson agreed to serve as president of the newly formed company—Advanced Diagnostics. Within five years from the time of its formation, the company became insolvent. The reason for the failure was that Dr. Atkinson did not know what business he was in.

Dr. Atkinson appeared to be uniquely qualified to head up the new company. As department head in the medical college of a major university, he had established an international reputation in medical diagnosis. He was one of those special individuals who was fluent in both computer science and medical science. By combining these two disciplines, he was able to develop procedures that were on the leading edge of medical diagnosis.

Dr. Atkinson was a medical researcher *par excellence*. Any professional meeting dealing with medical diagnosis invariably would feature Dr. Atkinson as a keynote speaker. He had published some 30 papers in professional journals and was now working on a textbook that his associates believed would serve as the "bible" for medical diagnosis. He also had some 20 patents that were jointly held with the university.

It was Dr. Atkinson's brother-in-law, Ben, who saw the market potential for Dr. Atkinson's work. As an entrepreneur, Ben envisioned a company that would develop and market advanced diagnostic equipment. With Dr. Atkinson's professional knowledge providing the technical base and Ben's contacts with potential investors providing the financial base, Ben was convinced that he could be successful.

When Ben broached the subject with his brother-in-law, there was only a mild response. But Ben persevered. He did a detailed financial analysis that included a return-on-investment projection over a 10-year period. When Dr. Atkinson was shown these figures, he was impressed. Based on Ben's analysis, it appeared that, within five years, Dr. Atkinson could be earning at least twice what the university was paying him. With four children to get through college—and perhaps even medical school—this additional income could be put to excellent use.

Dr. Atkinson then agreed to go with Ben to discuss the matter with the dean of the medical college. When Ben presented the ROI analysis to the dean and suggested that the medical college would share in the company's profits in exchange for releasing the jointly-held patents, the dean expressed considerable interest.

Within two weeks, the dean had obtained approval from the university's administration to proceed with the plan. And to Dr. Atkinson's pleasure, the dean requested that Dr. Atkinson remain on the staff as a part-time faculty member. Certainly an ideal arrangement: to be the president of a company that promised a substantial income, and, simultaneously, to remain as a member of the academic community.

Francis and Ben then proceeded "full steam ahead" to develop a detailed five-year plan for the new company. Francis focused on research and development, equipment and facilities, and staffing, while Ben focused on financial and legal matters. They agreed that there should be a board of directors comprised of three members from the medical community and three from the business community. The two brothers-in-law spent numerous evenings and most weekends developing the plan.

Ben was successful in obtaining the financial support needed to launch the new company. Potential investors who sat through Ben's presentation were convinced that Advanced Diagnostics would be a low-risk venture with outstanding potential for financial return. Within three months, Ben had gotten commitments for the $2,500,000 that he had set as the target.

Exactly one year after Ben had first proposed the idea to his brother-in-law, the new company was launched. The facility was small but elegant. All of the equipment included in the five-year plan had been purchased and installed. And ready to go to work were six eager staff members: two medical researchers, a computer specialist, an equipment designer, a technician, and a secretary.

The transition from the world of academia to the world of business was fairly smooth for Dr. Atkinson. The laboratory that he had established in his new company, while somewhat more advanced, was practically a replica of that which he had in the university. This new laboratory would allow him to continue the work that he was doing at the university.

Dr. Atkinson was able to create an organizational climate for his staff that was intellectually stimulating. Every Friday, he held a two-hour seminar for the entire staff in which he led a discussion on some specific aspect of medical diagnosis. Inasmuch as he was now heavily involved in writing the textbook on medical diagnosis, he would select as a seminar topic the particular chapter that he was working on at the time.

Dr. Atkinson took great pleasure in the fact that he was still an active member of the professional medical community. He went to the university one day each week to teach his class in the medical college and have discussions with his colleagues. And he continued to participate actively in professional meetings in the U.S. and abroad.

And so the operation continued for two years. But at the next quarterly board of directors meeting, there was a clash of viewpoints. Dr. Atkinson's review of the company's latest technical developments was applauded by the three board members from the medical community. But the financial report brought looks of annoyance from the three members from the business community. Even though the company was advancing the state-of-the-art in medical diagnosis, the financial picture looked dismal. The company was overspending by a considerable amount. But even worse, there were no customers beating a path to their door to purchase the new procedures and equipment. After a heated exchange and unpleasant debate, Dr. Atkinson agreed to develop his marketing plan and present it at the next quarterly board meeting.

At the summer board meeting, Dr. Atkinson's market plan was met with only lukewarm acceptance by the three members from the business community. The three members could now see that Dr. Atkinson was indeed an outstanding medical researcher and scholar, but he was no businessman. The board agreed that a marketing specialist should be hired immediately and that a more acceptable marketing plan should be presented at the next board meeting.

Finally, at the fall board meeting, the essence of the problem was identified. This was the gist of the exchange:

Board member: Tell me, Dr. Atkinson, what business are we in?

Dr. Atkinson: We are in the business of medical diagnosis.

Board member: But what *aspect* of medical diagnosis?

Dr. Atkinson: *Advanced* medical diagnosis—which is the name of our company.

Board member: But *what about* advanced medical diagnosis? What is our product?

Dr. Atkinson: We are developing advanced procedures and equipment for medical diagnosis.

Board member: Tell me, Dr. Atkinson, who is our customer?

Dr. Atkinson: The medical community, of course.

Board member: That response is too general. Who are our *specific* customers? Who will pay money for the procedures and equipment that you are developing?

Dr. Atkinson: The hospitals and medical practitioners.

Board member: What are you doing to cultivate these customers?

Dr. Atkinson: That's why we hired the marketing specialist.

One of the other board members then interrupted the exchange. Joan, a business person, summed up the issue very clearly: "I think I now see the root cause of our problem. We really don't know what business we are in. Dr. Atkinson and his staff have assumed that they were in the business of advancing the state-of-the-art in medical diagnosis—exactly what he was doing at the university. But the 25 investors, who have each invested $100,000 in the enterprise, have assumed that we were in the business of marketing the technology that Dr. Atkinson had developed previously at the university."

Frank, the third member of the business community, then commented: "I absolutely agree with Joan. It's an issue of being either technology-driven or market-driven. All along, Dr. Atkinson has been technology-driven—which was all right in the university. But, as president of our new venture, he should have been market-driven."

Sam, the board member who started the exchange with Dr. Atkinson, then exclaimed, "We don't even know the mission of our company! I think we are in big trouble."

During this entire exchange, the three board members from the medical community merely observed in silence. It seemed that, for the first time, these three members also realized that the company was in "big trouble."

Before adjourning, the board agreed to hold an emergency meeting in one month to try to turn the situation around. During the intervening month, the company's marketing specialist discovered that a competitor apparently had infringed on at least two of Advanced Diagnostics' patents. So a legal battle on this patent issue consumed Dr. Atkinson and the board for the next six months. They never *were* able to prove the competition guilty. But they were able to prove that they lost thousands of dollars in attorney fees and much valuable time in fighting the battle.

During the court proceedings, another competitor entered the picture with diagnostic procedures and equipment that could equal anything that Dr. Atkinson and his staff had developed. This company's procedures and equipment were tailored to the specific needs of the hospitals. This was a market-driven company that would gain 50 percent market share over the next five years.

From then on, Advanced Diagnostics continued to go downhill. The $2,500,000 initial investment plus a substantial bank loan were soon depleted, and the investors were told the bad news.

One month after Advanced Diagnostics was declared insolvent, the three board members who represented the business community met for dinner. This was a time for Frank, Joan, and Sam to commiserate. Toward the end of a rather somber evening, Joan posed to the other two this question: "What was the principal thing that we learned from this venture?" Frank responded, "Without a doubt: Before you start a new venture, make it crystal clear to everyone involved exactly what business you are in."

Sam then chimed in: "I would say that this was a pretty expensive learning experience. What it cost each of us is just about the same as what it's now costing me to put my daughter through four years at Harvard."

Knowing the World

We have learned that we cannot live alone, at peace; that our own well-being is dependent on the well-being of other nations far away. We have learned that we must live as human beings, and not as ostriches, nor as dogs in the manger. We have learned to be citizens of the world, members of the human community.

Franklin Delano Roosevelt
Quotations from Our Presidents

＊

$\mathcal{T}$om is the manager of marketing for a large industrial firm in Ohio. He has just returned from a 10-day marketing trip to Tokyo with his manager. His wife, Sue, has driven to the airport to pick him up. This is the dialogue:

Sue: Hi! Welcome home! I missed you.

Tom: I missed you, too. I sure am glad to be back.

Sue: How did the trip go?

Tom: Well, I have good news and bad news. Which do you want first?

Sue: Let's hear the good news.

Tom: The outstanding part of the trip was that I got an education in Japanese culture. As you know, this was my first trip to Japan. All that I had known before was based on what I had read and heard. But there's nothing like first-hand experience. I now feel that I have a much better understanding of the Japanese—their culture, their values, and how they think. And all of this at company expense.

Sue: Then what is the bad news?

Tom: We blew it.

Sue: You blew it?

Tom: We truly blew it.

Sue: How do you mean?

Tom: Well, as you know, the Japanese firm that we visited invited us to come to their headquarters to discuss our products and services. They invited us! We were their honored guests. What a fantastic opportunity!

Sue: What a nice position to be in.

Tom: You bet. But we blew it.

Sue: I can tell that you are upset.

Tom: I am *very* upset.

Sue: Why don't you start at the beginning.

Tom: Well, our Japanese host set up our schedule so that Marty and I would have Monday and Tuesday to get to know their operation and then to meet with their top-management people for an all-day session on Wednesday.

87

Sue: That makes sense.

Tom: Sure. And the first two days went extremely well. We had an opportunity to really learn about their overall operation in that two-day period. And Marty and I were convinced that they had a definite need for our products and services. There appeared to be a perfect match.

Sue: Then what happened on Wednesday?

Tom: That's the sad part of the story. The bottom line is that we simply were too aggressive for the Japanese. We were too eager to make a big sale.

Sue: It's a different culture.

Tom: It sure is. I wish that we had known then what we know now.

Sue: What actually happened in the Wednesday meeting?

Tom: As director of marketing and sales, Marty took the lead in the meeting. I was there to assist him. He gave a nice presentation at the beginning of the session—with overhead transparencies and all. And he did a pretty good job in showing them that we understood their needs.

Sue: That is commendable.

Tom: I agree. But during the discussion period is when the meeting started going downhill. This is when the differences between the two cultures began to show up. The Japanese have a tendency to nod their heads—and Marty interpreted nodding as agreement. Actually, they were responding that they *understood* what was being said—not that they agreed with it. So Marty was taking all the nodding as positive feedback, and he led them right up to the contract-signing stage.

Sue: Which was premature.

Tom: Exactly. And things simply got worse after that. The Japanese—in a very polite manner—proceeded to bring the meeting to a close.

Sue: What did your Japanese host say?

Tom: Essentially, "Don't call us. We will call you."

Sue: That is a very sad ending.

Tom: It is indeed. And what's really sad is that we have the products and services to meet their needs.

Sue: Well, I guess you can chalk it up as a learning experience.

Tom: I know. But that sure was an expensive learning experience.

The basic problem in this vignette is that Marty is afflicted with a serious case of "cultural myopia"—which is common among American managers. Myopia is defined as "a condition in which the visual images come to a focus in front of the retina of the eye resulting in defective vision." Cultural myopia may then be defined as "a condition in which one views the world through the contracted lens of one's own culture, which often results in narrow-mindedness, prejudice, and bigotry."

How do we overcome the malady of cultural myopia? The late Dag Hammarskjöld, former Secretary General of the United Nations, provides an answer:

> Everybody today, with part of his being, belongs to one country, with its specific traditions and problems, while with another part he has become a citizen of the world which no longer permits national isolation. Seen in this light there could not be any conflict between nationalism and internationalism, between the nation and the world.
>
> (in Kelen—*Hammarskjöld*)

Indeed, each of us can be a citizen of the world—in our outlook on life. Just as we are simultaneously citizens of a particular state and citizens of the country, we can be both citizens of our country and citizens of the world. Such an attitude would help cure the myopia.

But few leaders perceive themselves as being part of the mainland of humanity. They still reside on small islands dispersed throughout the world. They still refer to "Us" and "Them." They still have outdated perceptions.

Effective leaders of the future will be citizens of the world. Without sacrificing their own national loyalties, they will transcend these allegiances by also becoming world citizens. As world citizens, they will have a different viewpoint than other leaders who see themselves solely as citizens of their respective nations.

In terms of attributes, the citizen of the world:

- Identifies with the human race, as a member of the human community. The citizen of the world is a member of a local community, a state, and a nation. But, in addition, this person has taken the next step—which is a quantum leap—to becoming a member of the human community.

- Understands the interdependence of the world's nations. What happens financially in Japan will have an impact on the U.S. What happens politically in Europe will have an impact on the U.S. What happens environmentally in Canada will have an impact on the U.S. The effective leader fully grasps these interconnections.

- Studies other cultures through reading and travel. Through systematic study and firsthand experience traveling to other countries, the effective leader makes a special effort to become acquainted with the people, language, mores, and culture of the country.

- Communicates effectively with people of other cultures. The leader of the future, when planning to visit another country for an extended period of time, will participate in a "total immersion" program to learn the language of the country.

- Treats people of other cultures as equals. This person agrees with Sidney Jourard when he says: "There is no longer a category of Them; there is only Us."

As citizens of the world, the effective leaders of the future will make many contributions. But one in particular deserves special note: They will contribute to the ultimate aim of *the unity of humankind.*

V

CORE LEADERSHIP FUNCTIONS

A person's real values have a subtle but inevitable way of being communicated, and they affect the significance of everything he or she does. These are the vague intangibles — the "skyhooks" — which are difficult to verbalize but easy to sense and tremendously potent in their influence. They provide a fundamental structure into which the experiences of every day are absorbed and given meaning.

O. H. Ohmann
"Skyhooks"

The effective leader is committed to basic beliefs that guide his or her life. This leader has moved up the Ladder of Human Potential beyond the rungs of Coping and Knowing to that of Believing. As the third rung of the ladder, Believing provides direction for the lower rungs of Knowing and Coping.

The effective leader is *value-driven*. Clear values penetrate and are conveyed in the leader's words and actions. Much of the leader's time and energy are devoted to translating the values into practice.

Importantly, the effective leader is able to elevate the values of followers. The leader does not stop with the knowledge of a follower's present values. Leadership strategy involves elevating these values to ever higher levels.

Recall Abraham Maslow's five-tiered hierarchy of human needs: from physiological to safety to belongingness to self-esteem to self-actualization. What the effective leader does is facilitate the movement of each follower up the hierarchy, and, as a consequence, *new values emerge.*

With "Believing" serving as the encompassing concept, the effective leader carries out six core functions:

- **Valuing**—having a good grasp of the organization's values and being able to translate these values into practice.

- **Visioning**—having a clear mental picture of a desired future for the organization or organizational unit.

- **Coaching**—helping others develop the knowledge and skills needed for achieving the vision.

- **Empowering**—enabling others to move toward the vision.

- **Team Building**—developing a coalition of people who will commit themselves to achieving the vision.

- **Promoting Quality**—achieving a reputation for always meeting or exceeding customer expectations.

The leader who is able to carry out these six core functions effectively probably will be a "very good" leader. And the leader who is able to integrate these six core functions into a unified strategy is very likely to be an "outstanding" leader.

Valuing

Let us suppose that we were asked for one all-purpose bit of advice for management, one truth that we were able to distill from the excellent companies research. We might be tempted to reply, "Figure out your value system. Decide what your company stands for." ... Clarifying the value system and breathing life into it are the greatest contributions a leader can make.

Thomas Peters and Robert Waterman
In Search of Excellence

⇒✳⇐

I have asked several hundred managers this question: "Does your organization have a formal statement of values?" The results are illuminating. About one third of the respondents state that their organizations have a written statement of values and they know exactly what these values are. The next third indicate they believe their organizations do have a written set of values but they do not remember what they are—or, at best, they may recall only one or two of the values. Then the final third state their organizations do not have a written statement of values. Thus, there are three discrete types of organizations: (1) those that have formalized their values and the values apparently are "for real"; (2) those that have formalized their values but they serve only as "window dressing"; and (3) those that have not formalized their values.

Managers operating in the second or third category should heed what Peters and Waterman say: "Clarifying the value system and breathing life into it are the greatest contributions a leader can make." From these two authors' excellent companies research, it is noteworthy that this is their number one recommendation.

In *The Nature of Managerial Work*, Henry Mintzberg stresses that "The manager serves as the focal point for the organization's value system." It is essential that the manager fully understand the value system and be able to translate it into practice. And Mintzberg adds: "The dissemination of values occurs in terms of specific statements on specific issues, not in terms of global preferences."

The great teachers of ancient times had a clear grasp of their own values. Socrates, Buddha, Confucius, and Jesus understood their values, they instructed others in the importance of values, and, most important, they lived by their values. Inspired by these great teachers, we are more attentive to such basic values as love, truth, freedom, equality, fairness, harmony, goodness, and wisdom. Exemplifying these fundamental human values in their own lives is their principal legacy to us.

Moving to the modern age, we find that successful leaders in business and industry have a clear grasp of values and are able to translate these values into practice. Thomas Watson Jr., the former president of IBM, stressed three core values: Customer Service, Excellence, and Respect for the Individual. Ray Kroc, the man who put McDonald's on the global map, preached four core values: Quality, Service, Cleanliness, and Value. And there are many other such leaders. Clearly, all great teachers and great leaders share an excellent grasp of their own values . . . and they live by these values.

Organizational values are beliefs about what is important to an organization. They are the core of a corporate culture—"How we do things around here." Values may be either explicit (formalized in a written statement) or only implicit (serving as an ever-present but unwritten code).

Every organization needs a written statement of core values. These values should then serve as the "musical score" for every member of the organization.

To achieve the real force of values, the organization's stated values and its operational values must be in harmony. The stated values are those that upper management has formalized in a written document. The operational values are the actual values that the staff perceive to be pivotal in guiding managerial decision making. These two sets of values must be congruent to have a positive impact on performance. So if you, as a manager, have the responsibility to assure that the organization's stated values and its operational values are in harmony, here's what you can do.

Learn the organization's value system. A formal statement makes your job easy. Otherwise, you may have to probe. Perhaps there is an organizational mission statement that includes specific values . . . or an annual report that mentions specific organizational values . . . or some printed speeches by the CEO that refer to specific organizational values. Whatever the source, make a list of what you consider to be the organization's primary values. Then confirm your list of values with others in the organization.

Clarify the values. Values such as Quality, Teamwork, Integrity, standing alone, are vague. Find out what behaviors define or at least illustrate the values. The figure on the following page serves as an example. Note the values for Sandia National Laboratories and the clear, operational statements for each value.

VALUES OF SANDIA NATIONAL LABORATORIES

QUALITY

- Conform to customer requirements for performance, cost, and schedule
- Explicitly plan for and achieve continuous improvement

LEADERSHIP

- Anticipate the needs of the nation
- Convey a vision
- Encourage creativity, innovation, and initiative
- Set the standard
- Be courageous
- Understand and manage risk
- Be driven by a desire to be the best

RESPECT FOR THE INDIVIDUAL

- Trust and empower the individual
- Treasure individuality and diversity
- Be sensitive to individual needs and aspirations
- Expect, encourage, and reward accomplishment

TEAMWORK

- Ensure shared values and focus
- Create internal and external teams
- Create mutual benefits, mutual respect

INTEGRITY

- Honesty
- Objectivity
- Candor
- Fairness

Figure 4. Illustrative Organizational Values

Translate the organizational values for your particular unit. When conducting a leadership seminar for the administrators in a hospital, I asked the participants to formulate values for their own departments—and do it in the light of the hospital's core values. "Innovation" emerged as a principal value for the research and development department. "Accuracy" emerged as a principal value for the pharmacy department. Everyone there agreed that Innovation should not be a principal value for the pharmacy department.

Incorporate the values into the unit's vision statement, its strategic plan, and its performance appraisal program. By incorporating the values into vital aspects of the unit's operations, you will move from the abstract to the concrete. The team members will begin to appreciate how the values are an integral part of the entire operation.

Communicate the values continuously. Whenever giving a presentation to your staff, refer to the values. Whenever asking team members about their progress, refer to the values. Whenever leading a team meeting, refer to the values. Translate values into practice via communication.

Make decisions in the light of the values. Should you go with alternative A or alternative B? Refer back to the organizational values. In making the decision, these values often will serve as the tie breaker.

Conduct an annual assessment. Any manager genuinely committed to the organizational values should answer this question: How close are we to achieving each organizational value? A straightforward way to answer the question is to conduct an annual survey of your staff and your customers. With a one-page survey form on which the values and descriptor statements are listed, the respondents can evaluate on a five-point scale how well each unit is achieving each value.

Live the values. Perhaps most important of all, you must live the values on a daily basis. You must embody the values in your thoughts, words, and actions.

Carrying out these eight actions will help you translate organizational values into practice. The abstract will become manifest in the concrete.

Accordingly, as your team members incorporate the organizational values into their daily lives, you should see:

- The social energy and *esprit de corps* that moves the organization into action
- A sense of common direction for all staff and guidelines for their daily behavior
- A focus on what is most important to the unit
- A framework for decision making
- Standards by which to gauge performance
- A sense of stability and continuity in a rapidly changing environment.

These are important achievements! Collectively, they can have a profound impact on the overall performance of your unit.

In sum, we should reflect on the words of the former president of IBM, Thomas Watson Jr.:

> I firmly believe that any organization, in order to survive and achieve success, must have a sound set of beliefs on which it premises all its policies and actions. Next, I believe that the most important factor in corporate success is faithful adherence to these beliefs. And finally, I believe that if an organization is to meet the challenges of a changing world, it must be prepared to change everything about itself except those beliefs as it moves through corporate life.
>
> Thomas Watson, Jr.
> in Pascale and Athos
> *The Art of Japanese Management*

➤✳︎⬅︎

Visioning

At its simplest level, a shared vision is the answer to the question, "What do we want to create?" Just as personal visions are pictures or images people carry in their heads and hearts, so too are shared visions pictures that people throughout an organization carry. They create a sense of commonality that permeates the organization and gives coherence to diverse activities.

Peter Senge
The Fifth Discipline

⇒✳⇐

*T*he principal difference between managers and leaders is found in vision. Managers wait for someone to give them the vision; leaders create the vision.

This key difference leads to other differences in performance. With respect to planning, for example, managers plan by extrapolating from last year's performance, whereas leaders plan by focusing on the vision. With respect to time frame, managers focus on the short-term, whereas leaders focus on the long-term. With respect to day-to-day activities, managers concentrate on solving today's problems, whereas leaders concentrate on those activities that will lead the group toward the vision. These are important differences in both attitude and behavior—and they have a profound impact on overall performance.

The effective leader has three interrelated attributes: the ability to create a vision; the ability to communicate the vision to others; and the ability to motivate and inspire others to work toward the vision. Simply having the vision is not enough.

A vision is a clear mental picture of a desired future. It articulates an engaging future for the organization. The vision statement may be as short as a single paragraph or as long as a 20-page treatise, but, in any case, it provides direction for the organization.

It is important to distinguish mission and vision. The mission specifies *why* the organization exists, and the vision articulates *what* it wants to become. The Materials Research Laboratory in Taiwan, for example, had this mission: to help meet the needs of industry through high-quality advanced materials research. This was the vision: to become internationally recognized for our high-quality research in advanced materials. Every organization needs both a mission statement and a vision statement.

Vision is of central importance to every person who holds a management position. This includes managers in marketing and sales, research and development, engineering, manufacturing, human resources, accounting and finance, facilities . . . everywhere. And it includes every level of management: first-level, middle-level, and upper-level. Every manager in the organization should have a clear vision for her or his organizational unit.

A good vision statement will satisfy several practical criteria. In developing a vision statement for your organizational unit, consider these criteria.

A vision statement should have a unifying theme. A first sentence like: "To become internationally recognized as a center of excellence for high-quality advanced materials research" is ideal. The remainder of the statement should elaborate this first sentence.

A vision statement responds to the needs of all stakeholder groups. This includes your customers, your staff, and your management. Here, your customers should be able to see their future needs being addressed. Your staff should be able to see their needs and aspirations reflected. And upper management should be able to see how the realization of the vision will add value to the larger organization.

A vision statement should provide direction for action. Albeit a vision statement is written in general terms, it nevertheless should provide direction for your team. It should clarify for all what their course will be.

A vision statement should be challenging yet attainable. If the vision statement is simply pie-in-the-sky wishful thinking, it probably will do more harm than good—by generating skepticism and perhaps laughter. But if it is written in the form of a "stretch goal"—one that is challenging yet attainable—it will have an energizing effect on your staff.

An illustrative vision statement is shown in Figure 5. This is the vision for Battelle, an international research and development organization. The statement satisfies the above criteria: (1) it has a unifying theme; (2) it responds to all stakeholder groups; (3) it provides direction for action; and (4) it is challenging yet attainable. (I think this is a good vision statement, but I could be somewhat biased. You be the judge.)

Given these criteria for assessing a vision statement, we can now delineate a systematic strategy for developing the statement. Consider the following six-step procedure and how you might adapt it to fit your particular situation.

THE BATTELLE VISION

Battelle will be a recognized world leader in providing value to our customers by solving significant problems through:

- Innovative participation in all phases of technology development—from conceptualization to commercialization
- Development and application of high value-added intellectual property
- Assignment of high quality staff, equipment, and facilities
- Collaborative relationships with our clients
- An open, information-sharing environment

Through this vision, we will achieve a leadership position in large and growing markets where our technology provides competitive advantages for Battelle and high value for our customers and society.

Figure 5. An Illustrative Vision Statement

1. **Identify the needs of your stakeholders.** Answer these questions: What are the projected needs of your clients or customers? What are the needs and aspirations of your staff? How can your unit add value to the larger organization?

2. **Identify a direction for your organizational unit.** No organization can be all things to all people. Focus is essential. What will be your unit's focus?

3. **Draft a preliminary statement of vision.** It is difficult for a committee to create a vision. To achieve unity in the vision statement, the first draft—or outline—must be created by a single individual. This, of course, is the leader's responsibility within each particular organizational unit. But by incorporating the information gathered in Step 1 of the process, the vision statement should unfold as a *collective* vision.

4. **Solicit inputs from your team and your manager.** With a draft

outline of a vision statement before them, your team members should be able to help you embellish and refine the initial statement. And your manager should be able to help you determine if the vision for your unit supports the larger organization's vision.

5. **Revise the preliminary statement as appropriate.** After soliciting inputs from your staff and your manager, develop an improved vision statement. In subsequent revisions, take care to keep the unity and integrity of the initial statement—unless, of course, you discover that the initial statement was flawed.

6. **Incorporate the vision in the unit's plans.** To translate vision into reality, incorporate the vision in the unit's strategic and tactical plans. The vision serves as the "driver" for the plans. By linking vision with strategy through systems thinking, you can assure a reasonable vision.

Heed the words of the bard:

> Vision without strategy is lame; strategy without vision is blind.
> But the uniting of vision and strategy reflects an integrated mind.

In sum, the central message here is that one of a leader's most important functions is to create a vision for the organization—a mental picture of a desired future. This vision should then serve as the lodestar for all other leadership functions.

> Truly inspirational leadership is not selling people some science fiction future. Rather, it is showing people how the vision can directly benefit them, how their specific needs can be satisfied. It is like holding up a mirror and reflecting back to them what they say that they most desire. When they see the reflection, they recognize it and are attracted to it.
>
> James Kouzes and Barry Posner
> *The Leadership Challenge*

Coaching

The real measure of the effectiveness of leadership at all levels is what is actually happening to the individuals directly responsible to that leadership — what changes are really taking place in the climate of the workplace, in the caliber of the people, and in the relationships of supervisor and supervised.

Lawrence Appley
Management in Action

⇒⟩⟨⟨⟨⟨

*I*n a meeting with a group of school administrators, I was stressing the importance of coaching. I suggested that one of the manager's most important functions was staff development and that investing time in coaching was sure to pay dividends in the form of a more capable staff. One of the administrators then asked, "But how will I get *my own* work done?" I replied, "Run that by me one more time." And he responded, "If I spend a large portion of my time coaching my staff, how will I get *my own* work done?" I then realized that I had heard him correctly the first time.

Many individuals in management positions have not made the vital shift from individual contributor to manager. Even though they hold the title of manager, they are still individual contributors. They view their primary responsibility as "getting their own work done." Consequently, coaching is not a significant part of their jobs.*

Consider two new employees: Carlos and Maria. Assume that they are approximately equal in overall ability and potential. Carlos is assigned to a manager who gives little heed to coaching his staff. Maria, on the other hand, is assigned to a manager who takes coaching seriously, who views staff development as a major part of her job. Now compare the performance of Carlos and Maria three years hence. In all probability, Maria will be far in front of Carlos—because her manager took coaching seriously.

A person learns a new job or new task in these three ways: learning on one's own, formal training, or coaching. But learning on one's own is not very efficient, and, further, learning the job the wrong way can be difficult to correct at a later date. Formal training is usually skimpy—with the typical exempt employee averaging only about three days of formal training per year. So that leaves us with coaching—on-the-job training provided by the immediate supervisor. Compared with

---

*Recognize, however, that in today's ever-lean organizations, many individuals are expected to be both a manager and an individual contributor. The either-or days are gone.

formal training, there are potentially some 220 days in each year when coaching could take place.

When it comes to coaching, the effective leader understands and applies Confucius' philosophy of teaching:

> The ideal teacher guides his students but does not pull them along; he urges them to go forward and does not suppress them; he opens the way, but does not take them to the place.
>
> Confucius
> (Lin Yutang—*The Wisdom of Confucius*)

As the Chinese sage says: "He opens the way, but does not take them to the place." The good coach does not give the answers. In fact, the leader as coach may not even *know* the answers, but can spur the thinking of individual staff members by posing thought-provoking questions—questions that might "open the way." This is coaching at its best.

One should evaluate the effective leader by the growth and development of his or her staff members. Lawrence Appley states it well: "The real measure of the effectiveness of leadership at all levels is what is actually happening to the individuals directly responsible to that leadership."

Do you consider yourself to be a good coach? Do you view coaching as an integral part of your job? Are you a developmental manager? To evaluate your own performance, try completing the 10-item survey in Figure 6. Answer each item on a 1 to 5 scale, with "5" being high and "1" being low.

If your total score is 40 or above, you probably are a good coach. You apparently view coaching as an integral part of your job.

Every day that you and your staff are together is a potential day for coaching. There is much that you can do.

Take the time to build a personal relationship with each of your staff members. Get to know them as individual persons. Find out their interests, their values, their aspirations. Find out what they want to accomplish, what they want to become. Explore with them their particular strengths and the particular areas in which they need to improve.

1. Has a grasp of the staff's present knowledge and skills.	_____
2. Knows what knowledge and skills will be required to achieve the unit's vision.	_____
3. Has a strategy for developing the needed knowledge and skills.	_____
4. Views staff development as a primary job function.	_____
5. Gets great satisfaction in helping others grow.	_____
6. Is able to diagnose performance problems.	_____
7. Takes mistakes in stride, as long as the individual learns from them.	_____
8. Takes a forward-looking approach in dealing with problems.	_____
9. Is authentic in giving feedback.	_____
10. Promotes lifelong learning as "a way of life" for all team members.	_____
Total score =	_____

Figure 6. The Developmental Manager

Easy to say, not easy to do. It takes a personal commitment on your part.

Give special attention to each staff member at the beginning of a new job assignment. You might have an individual contributor who has just been promoted to project leader. Or you might have a technical group leader who has just been promoted to section manager. These are events that call for your special attention. You need to spend time with the individual discussing the new assignment: requirements of the new job, pitfalls to avoid, and suggestions on how to succeed in the new job. Share your personal experiences with the staff member.

Use naturally arising interactions with staff to foster learning.

Some managers assume the role of teacher only during formal situations—such as during the annual performance review or during a formal lecture on a specific topic. This is a myopic view. Many everyday situations lend themselves to effective teaching and learning. A casual discussion with one of your staff members, for example, can provide an opportunity to reinforce a certain organizational value, raise a question about a given job assignment, or suggest a specific resource needed by the staff member. Be constantly attentive to learning needs; keep your antenna up.

Use work assignments effectively as a primary means of staff development. Under pressure, a manager usually takes on a rush assignment or gives it to someone who has done it numerous times. Such an approach—which is quite common for managers who constantly are working under pressure—helps no one grow. A more thoughtful approach calls for thinking through the various work assignments and giving them to individuals for whom they would be "stretch" assignments, that is, assignments that provide opportunity for growth. Individuals working under such an arrangement over a several-year period undoubtedly will experience considerable growth. The key is the manager's *thoughtful approach* to job assignments.

Master the art of delegation. One main reason why managers fail is that they never master the art of delegation. Some managers are convinced that they "can do it better" than their staff. Some believe that they do not have sufficient time to "explain it." And still others fear that they will "lose control." Whatever the reason, delegation is a major problem for many managers. Unless you master the art of delegation, you will not grow as a manager—and your staff will not grow.

Give honest feedback on a timely basis. Both learning theory and learning practice point up the importance of feedback. Without feedback, there will be very little learning. As a manager, it is your responsibility to give your individual staff members feedback on an ongoing basis—not merely during the annual performance review. The feedback should be specific, timely, and constructive.

Use performance appraisal as a means of teaching, not exhorting or punishing. In surveying several hundred managers, I have found that most of them dread the annual performance reviews with their staff members. They give such various reasons as:

- "I don't like to confront my staff about the negative aspects of their performance."
- "I feel that our forced-ranking system is demotivating to the majority of our staff."
- "I don't like arguing with my staff about the pay increases that go with specific performance ratings."

Unfortunately, many negatives are associated with the annual performance reviews. The key to turning the situation around is to establish a new primary goal for the performance reviews: *improving job performance.* These reviews should be to help each staff member grow and develop in the job. Every other purpose is secondary.

Indeed, many things you do can help your staff grow and develop in their jobs. Take coaching seriously. View coaching as a primary core function, not a mere peripheral function. View coaching as an integral part of your job.

Effective coaching has a multiplier effect. Consider, for example, a department manager who spends a great deal of quality time coaching her six group leaders. These six group leaders, because they have an exemplary role model, are likely to take their coaching role seriously with their own staff members. So the department manager, rather than impacting only six individuals, may now have a significant impact on some 50 or 60 others. By taking coaching seriously, you may leave a legacy.

> To the extent that leaders enable followers to develop their own initiative, they are creating something that can survive their own departure. Some individuals who have dazzling powers of personal leadership create dependency in those below them and leave behind a weakened organization staffed by weakened people. Leaders who strengthen their people may create a legacy that will last for a very long time.
>
> John Gardner
> *On Leadership*

Empowering

Motivating people for a short period of time is not very difficult. A crisis will often do just that, or a carefully planned special event. Motivating people over a longer period of time, however, is far more difficult.

John Kotter
A Force for Change

⇒≱⊱

*Y*ou may be one who believes that "empowerment" has become an over-used word. We come across numerous books and articles in the current management literature with "empowerment" in the titles. We receive brochures announcing seminars on "How to Empower Your Employees." And we review the criteria for Total Quality Management and find that empowerment of staff is a principal consideration. And so it goes. Granted that empowerment is a heavily used word, it nevertheless is a meaningful word. No better alternative word really captures its specific meaning.

Let's examine how empowerment operates in the everyday world. To illustrate its meaning, I have chosen a mundane example.

In the movie, "Five Easy Pieces," Jack Nicholson leaves a restaurant as an unhappy patron. Nicholson had joined several of his friends for breakfast. When it came time for Nicholson to place his order with the waitress, he said, "Toast only." The waitress replied, "We do not have 'toast only'. That is not on the menu." He could have ordered eggs and toast. Or he could have ordered bacon, eggs, and toast. But he could not order "toast only." So he ordered a chicken salad sandwich on toast and asked the waitress to leave off the lettuce, the mayonnaise, and the chicken salad.

Contrast Nicholson's situation to that of my friend Charles. I met Charles for breakfast at a restaurant in Colorado. The waitress took my order and then turned to my friend, "What may I serve you?" Charles responded: "I know this is not on the menu but I have a special request. Would you please give me one fried egg and one pancake." Without blinking an eyelid, the waitress responded, "Sure, no problem."

At a very simple and mundane level, we are talking about empowerment. The waitress who served Jack Nicholson was not empowered to deviate from what was specifically on the menu. But the waitress who served Charles was. The causal factor accounting for the difference between the one waitress and the other undoubtedly can be found in the training that they received—or the lack thereof.

After introducing the subject of empowerment to a group of 25 managers in a research laboratory, I was puzzled by the response. Almost in unison, these managers claimed that their scientists and engineers did not want to be empowered. As I probed with follow-up questions, I began to understand why the research staff were resistant to being empowered. For one thing, many of the staff apparently interpreted empowerment to mean that supervisors "would dump their grunt work" on them, that is, the routine administrative work that the supervisors did not want to handle. And second, there apparently were some research staff who did not want the accountability that goes with empowerment.

There are two different issues here. The view of "dumping grunt work" is simply a misunderstanding—or misapplication—of empowerment. But the issue of not wanting the accountability that goes with empowerment is a much more serious problem.

Put simply, to empower is to enable others to act. Power means the ability to influence others, to get things done. Even though the word "power" sometimes carries a negative connotation, it in itself is neither positive or negative. It depends on the intent of the power holder and how the power is actually used. For a manager or an individual contributor to get things accomplished in an organizational setting, power is essential. This being said, we can then define empowerment as "giving power to others."

To appreciate how empowerment can be a motivator, we need to contrast it with the more traditional motivation—namely, reward and punishment. These two approaches to motivation are radically different in both application and results.

Management has long relied on reward and punishment—or the carrot-and-stick approach—as the principal means of motivating employees. Hold out a carrot in the form of a possible pay raise, a promotion, or a desirable job assignment. Or hold out a stick in the form of a possible reduction in pay, a demotion, or an undesirable job assignment. This approach undoubtedly brings about "movement," but one can question whether or not this movement is the same as motivation.

Now we have a better approach to motivation—*empowerment*. But if empowerment means "to enable others to act," how is it accomplished? There are three interrelated aspects of empowerment.

As indicated in the "Empowerment Triangle" of Figure 7, the three essential requirements for empowerment are vision, resources, and

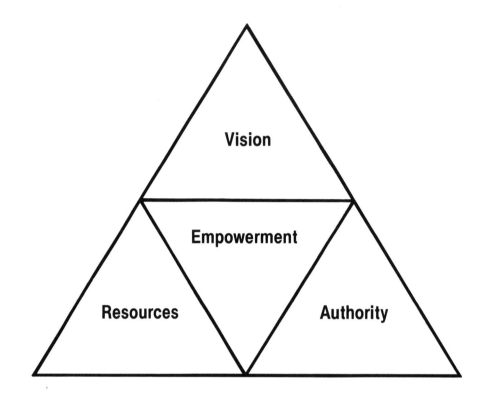

Figure 7. Essential Requirements for Empowerment

authority. The vision is the clear mental picture of a desired future. The resources are the tools needed by the individual to advance toward the vision—including knowledge and skills, support staff, equipment, money. The authority is the formal power invested in the individual to make decisions—namely, delegation. Lacking any one of these requirements, the individual will be disempowered. But holding all three, the individual will be empowered in the best sense of the term.

Given these definitions of basic concepts, we can now look at a comprehensive strategy for empowering staff. In his book, *A Force for Change*, John Kotter suggests a practical—and effective—approach.

1. **Communicate the vision on a continuous basis.** Some managers apparently believe that the presentation and discussion of the vision is a one-time event or, at most, a once-a-year event. It doesn't really work that way. To be effective, the vision must be communicated day in and day out, serving as a constant beacon for the staff. The vision should be a living force in the everyday lives of your staff.

2. **Communicate the vision beyond just informing; excite people by connecting it to their values.** A good vision statement will have coherence and commitment. Coherence means it has unity; it is all of a piece. Commitment means the staff have ownership of the vision; the vision taps into their values and aspirations.

3. **Encourage people's involvement in deciding real ways to implement the vision; don't be manipulative.** The vision describes "what we want to become" but does not describe "how we plan to get there." The vision is necessary but not sufficient. To complete the picture, there must be a written plan. The effective leader will work with the staff to develop a written plan, which becomes the road map for moving from the present toward the vision.

4. **Provide the right kind of support so that individuals can succeed in making progress toward the vision.** What kind of support can you provide? Here we are referring to the other two edges of the Empowerment Triangle: resources and authority. As mentioned previously, the resources are the tools needed by the individual to achieve the vision. The authority is the formal power delegated to the individual for decision making. This is genuine support.

5. **Offer sincere rewards and recognition.** There are numerous ways that you can recognize your staff for their efforts and their successful accomplishments in moving toward the vision. And you need not wait until some long-range goal is achieved. You can celebrate small victories along the way.

In these five guidelines, Kotter offers an effective strategy for empowering staff. They are not simply a random list of "how to motivate employees." Rather, here is a unified and workable strategy.

This being said, we now pose a salient question: Why is empowerment a more effective motivator than reward and punishment? Put yourself on the receiving end, and the answer is rather obvious. With reward and punishment, individuals on the receiving end often feel that they are being manipulated, that they are being treated as objects or things. But with empowerment, individuals on the receiving end usually feel that they are being enabled to act, that they are being viewed as responsible persons.

The differential results of the two approaches are convincing. With reward and punishment, we often find that individuals will do just enough to retain their jobs—no more and no less. But with empowerment, we often find that individuals will do their very best—they will "go the extra mile" to advance toward the vision.

Perhaps the most powerful aspect of empowerment is that it can motivate staff over a long period of time. It is easy to motivate staff over a short period of time—such as completing an important project on schedule or preparing for an audit team visit. But sustaining staff motivation over a long period of time is a completely different matter. The answer lies in the Empowerment Triangle: vision, resources, and authority.

> The essential thing in organizational leadership is that the leader's style pulls rather than pushes people on. A pull style of influence works by attracting and energizing people to an exciting vision of the future. It motivates by identification, rather than through rewards and punishments.
>
> Warren Bennis and Burt Nanus
> *Leaders*

116

Team Building

Team learning is vital because teams, not individuals, are the fundamental learning unit in modern organizations. This is where "the rubber meets the road." Unless teams can learn, the organization cannot learn.

Peter Senge
The Fifth Discipline

*I*n his book, *The Fifth Discipline*, Peter Senge enlightens us about the myth of the management team. You may agree with Senge that it is a misnomer to designate the typical management group as a "team." His remarks do not apply to all management teams but no doubt to a large number of them.

Senge asks us to consider the typical management team in a large organization. We have a CEO and some eight vice presidents. This group of nine is called "the management team." We see a neatly constructed organization chart with the name of the CEO at the top of the chart and eight boxes with the names of the vice presidents and their functional areas. All of these executives have offices on the fifth floor of the main building. They meet most Monday mornings in the executive conference room from 9:00 until 11:00. They all wear white shirts or white blouses and either dark blue or dark grey suits. Further, everyone in the organization refers to this group of nine as "the management team."

On the surface, this group of nine is a team. But when we penetrate a very thin layer of the surface, we find that this simply is not the case.

We find that each of the vice presidents is managing a "silo"—a vertical functional area. The silos are steep and have thick walls. The vice presidents see themselves as guardians of their silos, and that their principal responsibility is to protect their own silos and to ward off any threats or dangers posed by the other silos. There is little genuine communication between or among the silos, but no small amount of subterfuge. Occasionally, one silo will drain one of the others, and the two become one. And sometimes one of the silos will simply disappear, and there is no bereaving on the part of the other silo managers. This is the world of silo management. And on Friday afternoon the memo dispatched from the president's office will read: "The management team will meet in the executive conference room at 9 o'clock on Monday morning."

The effective leader is not a manager of silo managers. This leader can do remarkable things with silos: penetrate their thick walls, connect them, and even turn them on their sides. After a few adjustments here and there, they no longer look like silos but become more like interconnected tunnels.

The effective leader is able to build a genuine team of people who work collaboratively to achieve a common goal. Without a common goal, there is no team. Without working collaboratively, there is no team. Thus, the essence of "team" is found not in names or organization charts but in how a group of individuals actually *function.* If they work collaboratively to achieve a common goal, then we call them a team.

The effective leader builds a productive team that gets results over the long run. A very highly productive team will continue to get results even after the departure of the leader. As such, here are the attributes of a very highly productive team.

The members have a common mission. This team knows why it exists: to carry out the organization's mission. The mission clearly states the purpose of the product or service provided by the organization. The mission statement, which is written as a single sentence, is broad enough to include everything the organization does, yet specific enough to show how this organization differs from other organizations. Everyone on the team knows the mission and is guided by it.

The members have a common vision. All team members understand the organization's vision, which is a clear mental picture of a desired future. With the leader providing an outline of the vision, the members work together to fully develop it. This vision statement taps into the needs and aspirations of the individual team members, is future-oriented, and is very much present in the everyday lives of the team members. The tension between the vision and the present reality motivates the team members.

The members have a common set of values. While the mission describes the *why* of the organization and the vision describes *what it wants to become,* the values describe the principles by which it plans to operate. The values are the guiding beliefs of the organization, the guidelines for the daily behavior of the team members. Because the team members are genuinely committed to upholding the values, the *stated* values and the *operational* values are one and the same.

The members have a common strategy. This strategy is delineated in a written plan that serves as the road map for moving from the present reality toward the vision. The plan is a well-thought-out document that was developed collaboratively by the team members. It includes two parts: a five-year strategic plan and a one-year operational plan. The operational plan is reviewed on a quarterly basis and revised as appropriate. And each year, the strategic plan is extended one year into the future.

The members engage in honest and open communication. The team members speak the truth insofar as their thoughts, feelings, and words are congruent. There are no hidden agendas; what you see is what you get. It is this honest and open communication that leads to a high degree of trust between and among the team members.

The members feel free to express their individual opinions. This team knows how to blend unity and diversity. The unity is like the center of the circle: a common mission, a common vision, common values, and a common strategy. The diversity is found in the radii of the circle: the unique personalities of the individual team members. Without the unity, there would be no team. Without the diversity, there would be no life to the team.

The members deal openly with their conflicts. While some teams may view conflict as negative, the productive team views it as wholesome and essential because it is a conflict of ideas, not of personalities. Here the team members are completely free to express their individual ideas, and they expect—and accept—a clash of ideas. This clash of ideas leads to higher order ideas.

The members collaborate in solving problems and making decisions. When faced with an important team problem or decision, the members get together to deal with it. They discuss the issue, get all viewpoints out on the table, and usually achieve a resolution that is acceptable to all members. Two primary factors contribute to the early resolution of most problems and decisions. First, there is a commitment to the common mission, vision, values, and strategy—which provides the framework. And second, the members respect one another and truly listen to one another—which provides the context. This is teamwork at its best.

Once a decision is made, everyone supports it. When decisions will impact the total group, everyone on the team will not get his or her own way. During the decision making process, however, every member of the team will have ample opportunity to express his or her own views and to attempt to persuade the other members. After the discussion, the team usually will arrive at a consensus on a given alternative, and everyone on the team supports this choice.

The team IQ is greater than the average IQ of the members. Senge poses an astute question when he asks, "How can a team of committed managers with individual IQs above 120 have a collective IQ of 63?" Excellent question! But in the arena of management, it does indeed happen. The output of the management team—in the form of a decision or a problem resolution—may be far less than what was expected in view of the intellectual level of the individual members. But not so with the productive team. Here we find a team IQ that is at least ten points greater than the average IQ of the members. And the reason can be found in the principle of *team learning.*

How is it possible for any team to attain such a level of excellence? If we ask, "Is it *likely* that a typical team will ever achieve such a level of excellence?" Probably not. But if we ask, "Is it *possible* for a team to achieve such a level of excellence?" Definitely yes. Even though they may be few in number, such teams do exist. And if something *does* exist, then it *can* exist.

The question then becomes: What might you do to develop a productive team? To get started, here is a four-step strategy.

1. Evaluate your present team by use of the assessment inventory in Figure 8. (Evaluate each item on a five-point scale, with "5" being excellent and "1" being poor.)

2. Ask your team members to evaluate the team by use of the same assessment inventory. (And they should do it anonymously.)

3. Hold a one-day retreat with your team members in which you address a single question: What can we do to become a more productive team? (Use the results of the assessments as baseline data.)

4. Follow up on the recommendations.

This strategy can serve as one significant step toward developing a more productive team. For it to work, you must be sincere in soliciting feedback and recommendations from your team members. And you must

1. The members have a common mission. _____

2. The members have a commmon vision. _____

3. The members have a common set of values. _____

4. The members have a common strategy. _____

5. The members engage in honest and open communication. _____

6. The members feel free to express their individual opinions. _____

7. The members deal openly with their conflicts. _____

8. The members collaborate in solving problems and
making decisions. _____

9. Once a decision is made, everyone supports it. _____

10. The team IQ is greater than the average IQ of its members. _____

Total Score= _____

Figure 8. The Productive Team

follow up on the recommendations generated at the retreat. After you become comfortable with this approach to team building, you might find it advantageous to repeat the process on an annual basis.

What you are likely to achieve from your efforts is not merely a team, but a "learning team."

> Team learning is the process of aligning and developing the capacity of a team to create the results its members truly desire. It builds on the discipline of developing shared vision. It also builds on personal mastery, for talented teams are made up of talented individuals. But shared vision and talent are not enough. The world is full of teams of talented individuals who share a vision for a while, yet fail to learn. The great jazz ensemble has talent and a shared vision (even if they don't discuss it), but what really matters is that the musicians know how to *play* together.
>
> Peter Senge
> *The Fifth Discipline*

Promoting Quality

The single most important thing to remember about any enterprise is that results exist only on the outside. The result of a business is a satisfied customer. The result of a hospital is a healed patient. The result of a school is a student who has learned something and puts it to work ten years later. Inside an enterprise, there are only costs.

Peter Drucker
The New Realities

⇒✳︎⇐

*J*ohn took over the management of a division with serious problems. His challenge was to solve the problems in two years or less—or the division would be closed.

John was recruited from a competitor to serve as the vice president of the telephone switching division of a telecommunications company. This division was responsible for designing, manufacturing, and installing telephone switching systems. It was a vital part of the company's total operation.

The division was now "hurting." Having been in existence for more than 40 years, the organization had gone from "winner" to "loser." Before the deregulation of the telecommunications industry, the switching division had a captive market and showed a positive profit margin year after year. These were the "glory years." Then came deregulation and competition. That's when things began to fall apart.

John was recruited to head up the division because of his reputation as a can-do manager. In his 20 years of experience in the telecommunications business, John was well known as a manager who could take over an ailing organization and turn it around. And he would do it not as a Lone Ranger but as a team leader.

When John was in the final stage of the interview process, the company president gave him a challenge: Turn the division around in two years so it makes a profit. What a challenge! Why would anyone want to leave a high-paying secure job to move into such a high-risk venture? But John was "turned on" by challenges—and this one seemed perfect for him.

John, the new vice president, spent the first month on the job getting to know the organization. He toured the plant and talked with people. With every person he met, he asked questions and more questions. He never tired of asking questions. He listened attentively to the answers and he took notes. Before very long, he had a three-ring notebook filled with handwritten notes.

John spent the second month on the job getting to know customers—both present and previous. He asked these customers straightforward questions: What do you like about our product? What don't you like? If we developed a switching system that completely met your expectations, what would it be like? What is your view of the ideal switching system of the future? John listened attentively to the answers and he took notes. At the end of this series of interviews, John had another three-ring notebook filled with notes.

After studying and analyzing all the notes from these interviews, John was able to pinpoint the division's number one problem. It was obviously lack of quality—*as perceived by the customer.* For some 40 years, quality had been defined by the division's engineering department, certainly not by the customer. Inasmuch as the inner workings of a switching system were understood far better by engineers than by customers, why would anyone allow customers to define quality for them? For some 40 years this attitude had prevailed throughout the switching division.

With his homework completed, John held a landmark meeting with all of his managers. He was very explicit in describing present reality, the customers' views of the quality of the division's products, and the required turn-around in two years. He then proposed a paradigm shift: *to define quality through the eyes of the customer.*

As you might expect, there was initial resistance to this far-out notion—especially from the engineering department. But because of the urgency of their situation, most managers in the group eventually went along with John's proposal for a new definition of quality. And it was abundantly clear to everyone attending the meeting that, for the division to survive, there would have to be other dramatic changes.

John then launched an off-site five-day planning meeting with his 25 key managers. The purpose of this session was to develop a Total Quality plan for the division.

John's first major accomplishment in this meeting was to convince the managers that quality is free. Previously, these managers were convinced that every improvement in switching system quality cost a corresponding amount of money. But they had never really considered the cost of poor quality—in terms of rework and lost customers. Armed with data, examples, and logic, John convinced the managers that quality is indeed free.

The vice president's next major accomplishment was to get the managers to focus on "processes." He posed this question: Given our goal of meeting or exceeding customer expectations, what processes in the division contribute to this goal? This was a new concept for the managers, who previously thought only in terms of discrete organizational units and events. But process! What did he mean? Yet after John described specific processes and how these various processes cut across organizational units, the managers began to move with the flow—albeit a radically different flow than the one they had been entrapped in for decades.

The managers then spent an entire day identifying the various processes in the division that contributed to product and service quality. As different managers assumed the role of team leader, several whiteboards were soon filled with flowcharts. By the end of the day, the group had reached agreement on six different processes that probably had the greatest impact on product quality.

On the following day, the managers were divided into six interdepartmental process teams. Each team was to conduct an analysis of its designated process—to describe it by means of a flowchart, to determine the "value added" of each step in the process, to identify the high-leverage steps, and to pinpoint the constraints on each step. From this analysis, each team was to outline a plan of action for improving the process.

The next day, the leader of each process team presented to the total group the team's proposed plan of action. This was a day of rich discussion and dialogue. Each team benefitted from the inputs of the other members of the management group.

John ended the meeting with a call to action. His wrap-up presentation focused on three central themes: quality as defined by the customer, the need for constancy of purpose, and the absolute requirement for teamwork. When the managers left the meeting, they had a strange feeling—as did Dorothy in "The Wizard of Oz"—*that they were no longer in Kansas.*

Upon returning to the plant, the six process teams got to work in implementing their plans. Throughout this phase, each team held a weekly one-hour meeting to review progress, discuss issues, and plan next steps. John was always present in these meetings—unless he was out meeting with customers. Managers and employees throughout the organization were beginning to grasp the meaning of "constancy of purpose."

John held a monthly meeting with all 25 managers to review progress and discuss timely issues. Being a systems thinker, John was able to illuminate for the group the principal interconnections between and among the six processes that were being restructured and how the restructuring was having an impact on Total Quality. A significant outcome of these meetings was that the managers began to view themselves as something more than their jobs—they were indeed an integral part of a total system and each had responsibility for the total system.

An important action along the way was to celebrate small wins. With measures of performance clearly defined, it was possible for each team to track progress in its particular process area. Improvements in process called for celebration and special thanks to those responsible for bringing about the improvements.

And so the Total Quality program progressed up to the end of John's first year as division vice president. A trip to corporate headquarters to review the year's accomplishments elicited a considerable amount of deserved praise from the CEO. But the original mandate still stood: to remain open, the division had to become profitable within the next 12 months.

The breakthrough came at about midway into the second year. Installation of the new switching system was proceeding beautifully. There were practically no defects, because quality had been built in up-front. The system was meeting—and in many cases exceeding—customer expectations. The customers were delighted and word quickly spread to numerous potential customers.

Up to this point, all progress had been gauged in terms of process—not in terms of the end product. But the "proof of the pudding" was now found in fully satisfied customers.

At the next quarterly review meeting with the CEO, John was given the good news: the division would remain open. The division was still a little below the financial objectives set by the CEO, but there were enough new orders for the Number 8 system to assure considerable profitability over the next 18 to 24 months.

When John returned to the plant, they celebrated a success story in organizational change. And such success stories are not uncommon.

They are happening right now, everywhere, and they can start to happen in your organization today—if you have the will to make it happen.

What made John's story a success story? Consider these key factors:

- Initially, the division was "hurting."
- The new division vice president—John—understood and practiced Total Quality leadership.
- The managers were encouraged to try a new approach—defining quality through the eyes of the customer.
- The managers identified the processes that had the greatest leverage in impacting quality performance.
- A genuine team approach evolved.
- Constancy of purpose became a watchword.
- Excellent communication was a key factor in the changes.
- Celebrating small wins kept morale high.

Perhaps the most important learning that came out of the entire effort was the realization that quality improvement is a never-ending process.

> Changing a culture so that it never slips back is not something that is accomplished quickly. The process of instilling quality improvement is a journey that never ends.
>
> Philip Crosby
> *Quality is Free*

VI

CHARACTER

At every moment you choose yourself. But do you choose your self? Body and soul contain a thousand possibilities out of which you can build many I's. But in only one of them is there a congruence of the elector and the elected.

Dag Hammarskjöld
Markings

*W*ithin the Ladder of Human Potential, the effective leader masters the rungs of Coping, Knowing, and Believing. But the effective leader does not remain stuck at the third rung. There still remains an important step in the journey: the advancement to Being.

We now arrive at the level of existence that constitutes authentic selfhood. At the level of Coping, the individual's identity is immersed in actions and consequences. At the level of Knowing, it is immersed in common understanding of objective knowledge. And at the level of Believing, it is immersed in the ideas and values of a particular community. But nowhere up to this stage of development has the individual been revealed as a unique person, as an authentic self. Only at the level of Being do we find the individual revealed as a genuine person.

Within this hierarchy of levels of existence, the lower rungs of the ladder are given direction by Being. What one decides to believe is determined by Being. What one decides to know is determined by Being. And how one decides to cope is determined by Being. An appropriate metaphor is that Being is the gyroscope that guides you in your journey of self-development.

In advancing from the third rung of the ladder to the fourth rung, we note the principal difference between managers and leaders. Effective managers usually make it to the third rung. But by upholding the values and goals of their organization, they are reluctant to question these values and goals. Leaders, on the other hand, functioning as authentic selves, willingly call the organization's values and goals into question. And if done constructively and persuasively, they are recognized as leaders.

In essence, the fourth rung of the ladder focuses on the leader's character. Specifically, it includes six aspects of character:

- **Identity**—knowing who one is and who one is not, having a sense of wholeness and integration.
- **Independence**—being an inner-directed person rather than an other-directed person.

- **Authenticity**—revealing one's true being to others, maintaining congruence between the inner self and the outer self.
- **Responsibility**—being accountable for one's decisions and actions.
- **Courage**—affirming one's authentic being or essential nature despite obstacles.
- **Integrity**—being guided by a set of moral principles and being recognized by others as a person of integrity.

All six of these attributes are essential to effective leadership, but courage is most essential. Without courage, the other attributes are for naught. But *with* courage, the other attributes will be able to soar.

Identity

The exercise of leadership requires a strong sense of identity—knowing who one is and who one is not. The myth of the value of being an "all-around guy" is damaging to the striving of an individual to locate himself from within and then to place himself in relation to others. This active location and placement of one's self prevents the individual from being defined by others in uncongenial terms.

Abraham Zaleznik
"The Human Dilemmas of Leadership"

➤✳︎⬅︎

$\mathcal{I}$n their quest for identity, some individuals seem to lose their way. I want to tell you about three such persons.

I met Frank at a Christmas party. While conversing, I inquired about his line of work. He informed me that he had been retired for one year. His entire career was spent with a single company, a large manufacturing firm in the Midwest. In his 40-year career with the company, he had worked his way up from junior accountant to senior vice president. He held the position of vice president for the last 12 years with the company. Now, after being retired, Frank told me that he was experiencing an identity problem. When people asked him what he did, he didn't know how to respond—other than to say, "I play a little golf."

I met Charles in Kuwait. Charles was a British Ph.D. biologist who had been granted a two-year assignment with a research institute in this now well-known country. After being in Kuwait for some 12 months, Charles was undergoing an identity crisis. He had spent almost his entire life in a small town outside of London, and it was this community that provided him a sense of identity. It was this community that defined who he was. He informed me that he was under considerable psychological stress and at the time was receiving therapy from a professional counselor.

I met Ellen at a seminar. She was both a home manager and an insurance claims manager. Ellen especially liked the job of home manager—being a wife, a mother of two young daughters, and the current president of the school P.T.A. But she was only lukewarm toward her job as insurance claims manager. She had been with the company for 10 years and had successfully advanced from an administrative assistant position to the department manager position. What she liked about the job was the excellent pay, much of which was being invested in a college fund for her daughters. What she disliked about the job was the pressure placed on her to be and to act like the other managers— who were all males. She told me that she was unhappy.

All three of these persons were experiencing identity problems. But each case was different. Frank's problem was that his only identity was found in his position as vice president of the manufacturing firm. Once he retired, he lost his sense of identity. Charles's problem was that the locus of his identity was found in the external environment of the small community outside of London. When he left that community, he left his identity behind. Ellen's problem was that she was wrestling with two distinctly different identities—that of home manager and that of insurance claims manager. Because the two different jobs called for her to assume two quite different roles in life—to be two different persons— she was under considerable psychological stress.

Perhaps you can relate personally to at least one of these three cases. Most people experience an identity problem sometime in their lives. But the true test of character is not whether or not you experience such a problem, but how you deal with it.

The fully functioning person has a strong sense of identity. And the effective leader—as a fully functioning person—has a strong sense of identity.

> Identity is a coherent sense of self. It depends upon the awareness that one's endeavors and one's life make sense, that they are meaningful in the context in which life is lived. It depends also upon stable values, and upon the conviction that one's actions and values are harmoniously related. It is a sense of wholeness, of integration, of knowing what is right and what is wrong and being able to choose.
>
> Allen Wheelis
> *The Quest for Identity*

Along with Allen Wheelis, other psychologists and psychoanalysts have written extensively on the subject of identity. Their observations and insights provide us with a deeper understanding of this core attribute.

Identity is knowing who one is and who one is not. (Abraham Zaleznik) You are not born into this world with a ready-made identity; it develops over time—in fact, throughout your entire life. With respect to the direction in which you might venture, there are numerous possibilities. But at any given stage in this development, a firm sense of identity enables you to know who you are—as well as who you are not.

134

Identity is the experience that permits a person to say legitimately "I." (Erich Fromm) As you look at yourself in the mirror, you can say "I." And this "I" has real meaning. It is not "he" or "she" or "we" or "us." It is simply "I." It is the "I" that is the core of your self-being. And it is the "I" that distinguishes you from all other "I's."

Identity is the center from which one knows he or she plays different roles. (Rollo May) Each one of us plays a variety of roles in life: spouse, parent, child, manager, church member, club member, political party supporter, and on and on. Without a firm sense of identity, one might become entrapped in any given role—and allow that particular role to completely define the self. But with a firm sense of identity, our internal compass guides us in each role, and helps us realize that we are playing different roles in life.

Identity provides a sense of wholeness and integration. (Allen Wheelis) Without a firm sense of identity, we become simply the roles that we play in life. The self and the role are one and the same. Since each person plays a variety of roles in life, there would be a variety of selves. But not so with the fully functioning person. This person has a sense of wholeness that provides the integrative fabric for the various roles.

Identity is grounded in a hierarchy of values. (Allen Wheelis) Our values, our guiding beliefs in life, define who we are. The more values have been reflected upon and internalized in our self-beings, the more likely is our firm sense of identity. And the more these values have been prioritized, the more likely we are to have a firm sense of identity.

Identity is the ego's capacity to sustain sameness and continuity of essential patterns in the face of changing fate. (Erik Erikson) Through the years, you might very easily find yourself in many diverse environments: as you transfer from one organization to another, as you move from one city to another, and certainly as you travel from one country to another. And even in the same organization, you may find a radical shift in environments—say, if you get a new manager, or, say, if there is a radical shift from "good times" to "bad times." A firm sense of identity helps sustain sameness and continuity in these different environments. Even with the change in environments, you remain who you are.

Among these various aspects of identity, which together define a core attribute of the fully functioning person, how do you fare? How close are you to developing your own sense of identity? Whatever the case, you may benefit from the following suggestions.

1. **Write your personal philosophy of life on a single sheet of paper.** If you have never put your personal philosophy in writing, this will be no easy task. But it may be the most important thing you can do in defining and clarifying your identity—the person you desire to be or become. Include in this statement of personal philosophy three things: your life purpose (mission), your life goals (vision), and your guiding beliefs (values). After you have completed a first draft of the statement, study it and reflect upon it. Does the statement truly define the person you want to be or become? Does it define the *real* you?

2. **Live your personal philosophy on a daily basis.** It is one thing to write your personal philosophy on a single sheet of paper; it is quite another to live it on a daily basis. But this is your foremost challenge: to actually live your personal philosophy—both at work and at home and in bad times as well as good times. Live your personal philosophy so well that what is written on the sheet of paper and what is manifested in your daily life become one. "Put your theory into practice."

3. **Take a few minutes at the end of each day to reflect upon how well you lived your personal philosophy.** No one can be expected to have a perfect day. So evaluate and reflect. Ask yourself: With respect to my personal philosophy, what did I do exceptionally well today? Where did I go astray? What might I do differently tomorrow?

4. **Continue to refine and live your personal philosophy for the remainder of your life.** It is unlikely that you will have the same personal philosophy at age 60 that you had at age 20. You grow, you develop, you experience, you learn. And as you grow, you change. Update your written personal philosophy so that it reflects the person you are becoming.

These four suggestions are not a simple activity. They present a complex and demanding task—but perhaps the most beneficial thing you can do in your own personal development. It will help you develop a strong sense of identity, an internal compass that will guide your life.

A leader who has a firm sense of identity is likely to gain the admiration and respect of followers. There is a salient reason: predictability.

> A firm sense of identity provides both a compass to determine one's course in life and ballast to keep one steady. So equipped and provisioned, one can safely ignore much of the buffeting. Without such protection more vigilance is needed; each vicissitude, inner and outer, must be defined and watched.
>
> Allen Wheelis
> *The Quest for Identity*

Independence

We are fascinated by the growth of freedom from powers outside of ourselves and are blinded to the fact of inner restraints, compulsions, and fears, which tend to undermine the meaning of the victories freedom has won against its traditional enemies. . . . We have to gain a new kind of freedom, one which enables us to realize our own individual self, to have faith in this self and in life.

Erich Fromm
Escape from Freedom

⇒✦⇐

*I*ndependence is an essential attribute of the fully functioning person. In examining this attribute, we contrast two polar opposites: the Organization Man and the Effective Leader.

William Whyte Jr.'s Organization Man "sold his soul to the company store." There was an unwritten pact between the individual employee and the company—essentially, a social contract. The company would provide the job, a career, a monthly paycheck, and a reasonable amount of job security. In turn, the employee would give the company a day's work for a day's pay and complete loyalty. With loyalty would go conformity. The watchword of the day was "don't rock the boat."

For the individual employee, there was both good news and bad news. The good news was security; the bad news was loss of selfhood. There were some who considered this exchange to be fair. But I think it resulted in a great loss—for both the individual employee and the company.

Standing in sharp contrast to the Organization Man is the Effective Leader. This individual has a view that transcends the present reality of the organization. Within this view are found possibilities and potentialities of *what might be*. And it is the tension between *what is* and *what might be* that spurs the Effective Leader to bring into question many of the organization's present operations. As a result, the Effective Leader does indeed "rock the boat."

The fundamental difference between the Organization Man and the Effective Leader is found in the locus of control. For the Organization Man, the locus of control is within the organization, which means that the organization serves as the ultimate authority for the individual member. But for the Effective Leader, the locus of control is in his or her own self-being, which means that one's own conscience serves as the ultimate authority.

Abraham Zaleznik examines these two types of personalities in his paper, "Managers and Leaders: Are They Different?" He says the Organization Man is "once-born" and the Effective Leader is "twice-born." Once-born individuals "go with the flow." What the organization

139

is and what it *might become* are one and the same. So why question or challenge? Twice-born individuals, on the other hand, engage themselves mentally in a process that gives them two different perspectives. Mentally, they can be *in* the system, then *out of* the system, and then *back in* the system. This psychological process enables twice-borners to understand the present reality of the organization as well as other possible realities. This twofold view spurs the effective leader to question and to challenge the organization.

It is easy to see why some managers prefer to have a "subordinate" who fits the Organization Man model rather than the Effective Leader model. The former obeys and complies, whereas the latter questions and challenges. I believe that the enlightened manager will opt for the latter.

As Martin Buber says:

> Every person born into this world represents something new, something that never existed before, something original and unique.

Martin Buber
The Way of Man

Buber has a central message: You are unique. There are others with similar attributes, but no one is exactly like you. And in all of eternity there will never be another person exactly like you. Be proud of your uniqueness and nourish it. Here are several ways to nourish your uniqueness and sense of identity.

Learn to think like a philosopher. Philosophy is not a subject reserved for professional philosophers. It is a subject and way of life that is open to every person who wants to pursue it. As a philosophical thinker, you will learn how to question—and realize that the questions are as important as the answers. You will learn that there are different modes of truth—common sense, objective truth, subjective truth, philosophical truth—each with its rightful place. You will learn how to hold your ideas "gently"—as new truths are uncovered. Most important, you will learn how to be an independent thinker.

Live from the core out. There are those who live from the outside-in. They see what is happening and what others are thinking and saying.

They conform. Not so with the independent thinker. This person is sensitive to what others are thinking and saying, but this is not the pivot. For the independent thinker, the pivot lies within.

Develop a personal style. You play different roles in life: manager, spouse, parent, child, club member, and so forth. Develop a personal style that cuts across all of these different roles. Develop a consistent style and stick to it. As Gordon Allport says, this becomes your "stamp of individuality."

Don't imitate. It may be tempting to identify a single role model—an exemplary figure—and attempt to pattern your entire life after that particular role model. It won't work; you can never be exactly like any other person. You can indeed learn from the great teachers, but you cannot be a clone. And even if you came close, you would lose something very precious: your own stamp of individuality.

Develop thoughts of your own. Study the various issues of the day and how different individuals or authorities view these issues. Make up your own mind. Then be willing to express your own views on the various issues. This process helps you establish and reinforce your own individuality.

Develop your own plans. It would be so nice to just sit back, relax, and let someone else develop plans for you. For a continuing education plan, you could let a human resources specialist do it for you. For a career plan, you could let your manager do it for you. For a life plan, you could let your minister, priest, or rabbi do it for you. Don't succumb to the temptation. Seek the counsel of others but remain in the driver's seat in developing your own plans.

Be an active member of the team, but don't let the team prevent you from standing up for what you think is right. The effective leader is an independent thinker. But simultaneously with being an independent thinker, this person also is a good team player. The two roles are not mutually exclusive; they are complementary. Your challenge is to be a good team player *and* an independent thinker. This dual role is what allows you to make the most significant contribution to the team.

Assuming these guidelines become an integral part of your self-being, the result will be that you will become a twice-born person. You will be able to engage in a productive three-stage process:

1. Immerse yourself in a given system to understand *what is.*

2. Remove yourself psychologically to consider *what might be.*

3. Re-enter the system in order to help convert the *what is* into the *what might be.*

Understand that the Organization Man is locked into *what is* and never even considers *what might be.* The Victim considers *what might be* but only whines about it. This dysfunctional individual does nothing constructive to try to improve the situation. But the Effective Leader, as the third type, far surpasses the other two in both attitude and action. This productive personality understands present reality, attains an excellent grasp of possibilities for improvement, and then actively works at improving the situation.

Appreciate, however, that being an independent thinker carries both risks and rewards. The major risk is that you will be a threat to some managers, especially the true-blue Organization Man type. Your questioning and challenging certainly will not be welcomed by such individuals. And instead of receiving recognition and commendation for your independent thinking, you might encounter rejection and even dismissal. This is the real world. On the positive side, one of the greatest benefits of being an independent thinker is that it will help you establish a firm sense of identity.

> In proportion to the development of his individuality, each person becomes more valuable to himself, and is, therefore, capable of being more valuable to others. There is greater fullness of life about his own existence, and when there is more life in the units there is more in the mass which is composed of them.
>
> John Stuart Mill
> *On Liberty*

Authenticity

Whether or not we are aware of it, there is nothing of which we are more ashamed than of not being ourselves, and there is nothing that gives us greater pride than to think, to feel, and to say what is ours.

Erich Fromm
Escape from Freedom

⇒✱⇐

A dinner meeting with a college president gave me a great deal of insight into the relationship between authenticity and leadership. Cal and I spent most of the evening discussing the attributes of an effective leader. Cal told me that several years ago he discovered the most important attribute of an effective leader—*authenticity*—"being for real."

When Cal first became a college president, he *assumed the role* of a college president. And indeed it was a role. He acted as he thought a college president should act. But he wasn't himself. He was merely playing a role.

One year later, Cal realized that he was only marginally effective as a college president. Then he had an insight; it was like a "Eureka!" phenomenon. He instantly dropped the role-playing bit and simply became himself.

At first, this radical shift in demeanor was unsettling for his staff. But they got used to it—and they liked it. They sensed they were interacting with a *real person* now.

Cal was convinced that the main reason for his transformation was simply his new authenticity. He quickly established better rapport with all the persons he met. As he became more authentic, those around him became more authentic, too. His staff had also shifted from "play acting" to playing "for real." But it was no longer playing; it was actually living.

Cal also mentioned to me that one of the real spinoff benefits of being an authentic person was less stress. When playing the role of a college president, he had to be on guard constantly to make certain he was always projecting the "proper image." This was psychologically draining. Once he removed the guard, he could relax. He then experienced a sense of joy in his work that he had never experienced in his role-playing days.

I agree with Cal that authenticity is an essential attribute of effective leadership. But it is not the foolish authenticity that one sees in individuals who complete only Sensitivity Training 101. Without advancing to "201," these individuals believe that, to be fully functioning persons, they are to "let it all hang out"—regardless of the consequences. Not so with the effective leader. At a higher level of maturity, this person is a *responsible and courteous* authentic person.

Psychologist Carl Rogers provides an illustration of responsible authenticity. Rogers writes that he tried very hard to abide by this rule: "When anyone asks me what I think or feel, I give an honest answer. But there are times when I know that I should keep my mouth shut—because no one asked me for my opinion." I think this is a good rule.

Authenticity is the congruence between the inner self and the outer self. The inner self is the abode of your thoughts and feelings. The outer self is manifested in your words and actions. Inner self and outer self will be all of a piece. Here are some examples:

- Choosing to be fully known to others (Sidney Jourard)
- Saying what one thinks and feels (Martin Buber)
- Being spontaneous and unrehearsed (Erich Fromm)
- Refusing to deny one's experience and convictions "for the sake of peace and quiet" (Dag Hammarskjöld)
- Reducing phoniness toward the zero point (Abraham Maslow)
- Building bridges to others through being one's own self (Carl Rogers).

If, in your freedom to decide whether or not you will be an authentic person, your decision is affirmative, I can offer several suggestions for your consideration.

Be yourself rather than the role you play. You may be a college president, a director of a research institute, a manager at McDonald's, a principal of a high school, a department manager in a company, or what have you. Certainly, you desire to do a quality job in fulfilling that role. But don't *be* that role. Be yourself. Be your own self—a person with an identity that transcends the job position.

Communicate the present reality. Be honest in communicating the present reality to your staff. They deserve to know how the larger organization is faring and how your particular unit is faring at any given time. They also deserve to know the realistic projections for the future. Tell them both the good news and the bad news.

Communicate your expectations. Let your staff know exactly what you expect of them, both as a group and individually. Define clearly what you mean by quality performance, both conceptually and operationally. Give your staff some latitude in deciding how to get there, but be certain there is no ambiguity regarding the desired end result.

Give honest feedback to your staff. One of the most common disservices that managers do to their staff is to not give them honest feedback on their performance. It's fairly easy—and even enjoyable—to give positive feedback. But when negative feedback—constructive criticism—is needed, many managers remain silent. A given employee may proceed for years receiving an annual performance evaluation of "Fully Satisfactory"—without realizing that there are specific areas needing considerable improvement. Don't do this to your staff. Level with them.

Have the courage to confront. No two people can be expected to think exactly alike, so expect divergent views on a given issue. When you have ideas that diverge from those of your staff, your peers, or your manager, or if someone is creating a problem for you, confront the person. Attack the problem rather than the person. And engage the person in a problem solving session.

Welcome feedback from your staff. Your staff probably can give you more useful feedback on your performance than your manager can. They possibly see you more frequently than your manager and are in a better position to observe salient aspects of your behavior. Welcome this feedback. Truly listen to them and don't be defensive. And act on their suggestions for improvement.

Admit your mistakes. If you err and don't admit it, you are making a second mistake. Anyone who takes some risks will inevitably make some mistakes. The manager who is making no mistakes probably is not taking enough risks. You will never bat 1,000. When you make a mistake, admit it to your staff and your manager. And point out the lesson learned from the mistake.

Create a climate for authentic dialogue. In daily interactions and group meetings with your staff, you can create a climate for authentic dialogue. Communicate through your words and actions that it's okay to be yourself, to openly express your thoughts and feelings or express divergent views. And it is definitely okay to be a good listener. This type of environment is essential if you desire to develop a genuine "learning team."

These guidelines are not hard-and-fast rules. Think about how you might incorporate them in your own leadership style. I believe that they can help you become a more authentic person and, in turn, a more effective leader. But be aware that authenticity is fraught with both risks and rewards.

The major risk in being an authentic person is that you may be a threat to some individuals. There are many managers who live continuously in a world of facades. They wear masks and they "project images." Entire management teams are made up of such individuals. An authentic person who meets with or joins such a group is likely to be disruptive. A person who "says it like it is" is very likely to be viewed as a threat.

The major benefit associated with being an authentic leader is that you will gain the respect of your staff. They will know who you really are and won't have to waste their valuable time trying to figure out who you really are. They will know that you will level with them and, in turn, that they can level with you. The trust that results is the essential bond that unites the team.

A second benefit of being an authentic person is that it will help you develop a strong sense of identity.

> Honesty characterizes the authentic person and enables him to create an identity, to communicate a real presence, and to establish authentic bonds with others. The individual increasingly comes to know who he is through the stand he takes when he expresses his ideas, values, beliefs, and convictions, and through the declaration and ownership of his feelings.
>
> Clark Moustakas
> *Loneliness and Love*

Responsibility

The healthy personality becomes aware of his finitude and sees his life and what he makes of it as his own responsibility, not the responsibility of others.

Sidney Jourard
Healthy Personality

Consider, if you will, a real-life scenario and decide how you would respond. Assume that you are one of five department managers reporting to a director in a given organization. Each department manager has four or five group leaders reporting to him or her.

The management team—the director and the five department managers—has been discussing and debating a particular issue for several weeks. It is now time to decide between alternative A and alternative B; it has to be one or the other. The outcome of the decision will have a major impact on the entire organization. *Your group leaders are hoping that the management team will opt for alternative A.*

The team now meets to make the final decision. Each of the two alternatives is explored in depth and evaluated in the light of the organization's overall mission. Each department manager is given ample opportunity to express his or her own views about the issue. After the detailed analysis and discussion, *the team as a whole reaches a consensus on alternative B.*

You now return to meet with your group leaders, who are anxiously awaiting to hear the outcome of the meeting. What would you say to them? And how would you say it?

This is a rich scenario for distinguishing the Victim and the Effective Leader. These two types of individuals respond to this situation in radically different ways.

These are typical Victim responses:

- "Well, we lost another one."
- "They wouldn't listen to me."
- "I think they already had their minds made up."
- "They simply don't understand the *real* problem."
- "They don't understand *our* situation."
- "I don't think they understand the implications of their decision."
- "Basically, it boils down to politics rather than reason."

And on and on. The onus is shifted to the others, which lets the Victim "off the hook."

In sharp contrast to the Victim's response, this might be an Effective Leader's response: "Well, I know that some of you will be disappointed that the management team didn't choose alternative A. But we have decided to go with alternative B. We discussed both alternatives in depth and decided to go with B for these reasons: . . . Now it's up to us as a team—and as members of the larger team—to support that alternative." This is a responsible response.

The Victim and the Effective Leader stand as polar opposites on the dimension of responsibility. The Victim whines and complains; the Effective Leader copes. The Victim spends a great deal of time commiserating with other Victims; the Effective Leader spends time dealing with the problems. The Victim shifts the blame to others; the Effective Leader takes full responsibility for his or her decisions and actions.

There are at least two major problems associated with being a Victim. First, the individual who assumes this role is not very productive. And second, Victims who are in supervisory roles tend to bring others down—both in their outlooks on life and in their productivity. Overall, a professional Victim's contribution to the organization may very well be less than zero.

> Responsibility is the experience of being a determinant of what happens. Responsibility is the affirmation of one's being as the *doer* in contrast to the acceptance of the role of the *object* done-to.
>
> J.F.T. Bugental
> *The Search for Authenticity*

There is a world of difference between these two attitudes, and the one that you hold will have a profound impact on your effectiveness as a leader. Here's a collection of what a number of philosophers and psychologists say on the subject of responsibility.

Responsibility is realizing that you lay the groundwork for what you will be. (Karl Jaspers) Five years from now, you will be different from the person you are today. And in 10 years, you will be different from the person you will be five years from now. Why? Certainly there will be environmental forces and chance factors. But the principal determinant will be the decisions that you make along the way. What you will be as a person five years from now will be determined principally by what you are today and the decisions that you make between now and then.

Responsibility is being aware that one has the freedom to choose. (Immanuel Kant) Certainly everyone is affected by environmental forces that restrict freedom of movement and even freedom of thought. But every human being has a sphere of freedom, a domain in which one is free to choose. The fully functioning person—the one who has reached the top rung of the developmental ladder—is well aware of his or her freedom to choose. The pure determinists may try to convince you otherwise, but pay them no heed. As Kant duly noted, unless we accept the premise of freedom of choice, the individual could not be held responsible and therefore could not be morally good or evil.

Responsibility is being faithful to one's convictions. (Dag Hammarskjöld) The fully functioning person is guided daily by a set of principles and convictions, which serve as the internal gyroscope for showing the way, regardless of external pressure. These principles and convictions have been thoroughly incorporated into the person's self-being.

Responsibility is taking a stand before any new situation, encountering it, and responding with one's total being. (Martin Buber) Don't consult a rule book when a situation confronts you. You are in situations day in and day out, and move among them. Some situations barely enter your consciousness, while others may be life-threatening. Whatever the case, the responsible person confronts each new situation and responds appropriately.

Responsibility is putting one's self into the little things in life as well as into the big things. (Karl Jaspers) It is tempting to just do heroic acts and let everything else lapse. But you also are responsible for the small issues, too. Your effectiveness depends on both the big things in life and the little things.

Responsibility is being accountable for one's decisions and their consequences. (J.F.T. Bugental) Responsible persons are willing to be held accountable for the decisions they make. They knowingly make their decisions freely and, for good or ill, are willing to stand behind the decisions. And they also are willing to be held accountable for the consequences of their decisions. They do not try to shift the blame to others.

Responsibility is realizing that one can be accountable for inaction as well as action. (John Stuart Mill) Many of us believe that we are accountable for our actions. But we also are accountable for our inaction, which also can cause harm.

Responsibility is admitting one's mistakes and correcting them. (Confucius) To make a mistake and admit that you made the mistake is a sign of responsibility. To make a mistake, to admit it, and then to correct it is a sign of even greater responsibility. The leader who demonstrates this type of responsibility gains the respect of others.

These salient aspects of responsibility revolve around Bugental's notion of being the *doer* in contrast to the acceptance of the role of the *object* done-to. To be an effective leader, it is essential that you be a responsible leader. Here's how.

1. Don't be a Victim. Review your experiences over the past 12 months and identify those times when you assumed the role of a Victim. Can you think of a more appropriate nonvictim response in those situations? Make a commitment to snuff out any remnants of the Victim mode that still remain in your self-being.

2. Establish and maintain a reputation for being a dependable person. Whenever you make a commitment, follow through on it. Period. If you have some doubt as to whether or not you can do it, then don't make the commitment. Or at least clarify your constraints to the other person.

3. Be true to yourself. As a dependable person, you will respond to *external demands*. As a fully functioning person, you will respond to your conscience—the *internal demands*. Sometimes these two different types of demands come into conflict. When they do, listen to your conscience.

Freedom and responsibility are complementary concepts. Freedom presupposes responsibility, and responsibility presupposes freedom. One without the other results in a caricature of human potential.

In your freedom, be responsible. Don't be a Victim; be dependable; and be true to yourself. Remember:

> This inseparable relation of self and world also implies *responsibility*. The term means "responding," "response to." I cannot, in other words, become a self except as I am engaged continuously in *responding* to the world of which I am a part.
>
> Rollo May
> *Psychology and the Human Dilemma*

Courage

The word courage comes from the same stem as the French word coeur, meaning "heart." Thus, just as one's heart, by pumping blood to one's arms, legs, and brain, enables all the other physical organs to function, so courage makes possible all the psychological virtues. Without courage other values wither away into mere facsimiles of virtue.

Rollo May
The Courage to Create

154

━━✠━━

$\mathcal{E}$milie had everything going for her. At least, so it seemed. Then everything fell apart.

On the surface, Emilie appeared to be a fully functioning person. As a mother and a director of research, her *identity* was that of a successful leader-manager. As a nationally recognized leader in medical research, she was known for her *independent thinking*. As an up-front type person who openly expressed her thoughts and feelings, she would get high marks on *authenticity*. And as a dependable person who always fulfilled her commitments, she was recognized by her associates as a highly *responsible person*. With these four key attributes well in place, where did Emilie fall down? Please read on.

Emilie had 15 years' experience with the Nu-Drug Company, an internationally known pharmaceutical company. With a Ph.D. from Harvard in medical research, Emilie was placed on the fast track shortly after she joined the company. After establishing an international reputation for her advanced research in viral immunology, she moved into the management ranks. In a period of six years she advanced from technical group leader to department manager to director of research. And with all of this responsibility, she was still able to devote considerable time to her husband and two teenage daughters.

During the past five years, Emilie's research focused on developing a drug that would hold the AIDS virus in remission. With a substantial budget and several outstanding researchers, the project team was able to make considerable progress. Three years previously, her research team developed a drug—eeC—that showed great promise. If used in combination with the primary AIDS drug, zidovudine, commonly known as AZT, eeC should be able to hold the deadly virus in check.

Two years previously, the Food and Drug Administration gave conditional approval to test the new drug at three different sites. Because of the positive results from the pilot tests and the expressed support from the FDA, the company decided to drive "full steam ahead" in promoting and producing the drug.

At this point in time, Nu-Drug had invested almost $20,000,000 in R&D and another $4,000,000 in promoting and producing the drug.

155

But with annual sales expected to be at least $10,000,000, the company would surely realize a substantial return on its investment.

Unfortunately, the company was now in trouble financially. Because of a general economic downturn and the sudden emergence of additional competitors, the company projected a major financial loss for the year. But if the company could generate $10,000,000 in sales from eeC its first year on the market, it would end up in the black. Thus, everything hinged on the success of the new drug.

The president and the directors worked as a team in preparing to launch the new drug. As president of the company, Frank had given top priority to the development of eeC and provided the necessary resources. As director of research, Emilie had done an exemplary job in translating an idea into a useful product. As director of marketing, Charlie had promoted the drug both in the U.S. and abroad. As director of production, James gave top priority to manufacturing the drug in large quantities. And as the company lobbyist, Ernie had established excellent liaison with the FDA.

No one of these individuals could have done the job alone. But collectively, they did an outstanding job in taking an idea from its embryonic state and transforming it into a product that promised to save thousands of lives—as well as generate millions of dollars in profit for the company.

The company was now ready to distribute large quantities of eeC, pending FDA approval. It was then that Frank, the CEO, called an emergency meeting with all of the directors. He had just heard that the FDA would deny final approval to market eeC in the U.S. Two of the test sites had just reported that the drug had side effects, which resulted in the premature deaths of several of the test patients.

This was a grim meeting. It was as though everyone on the team had just been struck by a thunderbolt. Five years in the making and the likely watershed for the company's success, eeC was now "going down the drain."

But all was not lost. Even though eeC could not be marketed in the U.S., the FDA could not prevent it from being marketed in all of the underdeveloped countries and in a number of the developed countries.

So began a phase of the meeting in which one could witness

rationalization at its best (or worst?). Frank stressed that the success—and perhaps even the survival—of Nu-Drug depended on distributing eeC. Charlie, the marketing director, suggested that, even though the drug might cause a few deaths prematurely, it would certainly save a far greater number of lives. James, the director of production, agreed with Charlie. And Ernie, the lobbyist, opined that the specialists at Nu-Drug were far more qualified than those at the FDA to judge the new drug's efficacy.

And what was Emilie doing during the discussion? Nothing. She realized that they were dealing not with a legal issue but with an ethical issue—but she did not speak up. She thought that, if a drug is not suitable for Americans, then it is not suitable for any member of the human race—but she did not express her opinion. She contemplated that a short-term profit for the company might result in a long-term disaster—but she did not express her concern. Emilie remained silent throughout the entire meeting.

You can imagine what happened next. Nu-Drug shipped large quantities of eeC to 15 different countries, with the label on the containers reading "This drug can hold the AIDS virus in remission if used in combination with AZT." Revenue from sales was outstanding for about six months. Then came the bad news: a number of patients around the world had died as a result of taking eeC.

An investigation by the U.S. press corps caused the demise of Nu-Drug. An article in a major New York newspaper described in detail how the company had ignored the FDA warning and decided to market the drug anyway. The reader got the impression that Nu-Drug was an unethical company bent on exploiting AIDS victims in the underdeveloped countries. Included in the article were the names and titles of the five members of the management team.

Emilie was then faced with the difficult task of explaining to her family what had happened. She told her husband and two daughters about the crisis meeting that Frank had called. She then said to them, "The bottom line is that I didn't have the courage to speak up—even though I know that I should have."

This is a sad story and it had a sad ending. In slightly different form and with different characters, the story has been told many times.

If Emilie says that she lacked courage, the question then becomes: What is courage? Try this definition:

> Courage is the affirmation of one's essential nature, but it is an affirmation which has in itself the character of "in spite of." It includes the possible and, in some cases, the unavoidable sacrifice of elements which also belong to one's being but which, if not sacrificed, would prevent us from reaching our actual fulfillment.
>
> Paul Tillich
> *The Courage to Be*

To truly understand what Tillich says, let's consider some of his basic ideas one by one.

Courage is the affirmation of one's authentic self. You have an inner self that only you really know. This is your authentic self. You also have an outer self that is projected to others. This is your persona. The person of courage asserts his or her authentic self.

Courage is the affirmation that is made "in spite of." In affirming your authentic self, you will sometimes encounter obstacles and resistance. There are some individuals who do not want you to be your authentic self; they would prefer that you would be like them. There are some individuals who are threatened by your authenticity; they may reject you. But in spite of such obstacles, the person of courage asserts his or her authentic self.

Courage involves sacrificing peripheral desires. Picture in your mind's eye a large center circle and then several smaller circles on the periphery of the center circle. The large circle represents your authentic self, and the smaller circles represent peripheral desires. For various individuals, peripheral desires might include being wealthy, having prestige, being accepted by others, being successful, winning at sports, and so forth. For the individual who lacks courage, the center of gravity for one's life can shift from the center circle to one of the peripheral circles. But not so with the person of courage. This person will sacrifice peripheral circles in order to maintain the center of gravity within the center circle.

In the act of courage, the most important part of one's being prevails over the others. The fully functioning person has a firm grasp of his or her priorities in life. This person knows what is very important, what is moderately important, and what is unimportant ... and sets a course accordingly.

Courage is the readiness to take upon oneself negatives for the sake of a fuller positivity. Most people are disturbed when they are rejected by others—especially when those who are rejecting them are their friends. And most people don't like to have their ideas dismissed by persons of knowledge. But the person of courage will bear the burden of such negatives for the greater good—namely, to remain an authentic person.

The courage to be as oneself is the courage to follow reason and to combat unreason. Daily, you are faced with external demands and pressures—some are rational, others are irrational. In some instances, going with the irrational would be the path of least resistance. But for the person of courage, the rational will be the touchstone. Moreover, rationality will be used to combat irrationality. We have seen this approach take form in the lives of such notable persons as Henry David Thoreau, Mahatma Gandhi, and Martin Luther King Jr.

The courage to be as oneself is the courage to make yourself what you want to be. You no doubt have two mental models of yourself: the person you now are and the person you truly want to become. The person of courage will make sacrifices and overcome obstacles in this journey toward becoming the desired self.

The Oracle at Delphi advised each person to "know thyself." Paul Tillich advises each person to "be thyself." And importantly: "Be thyself in spite of obstacles." *Have the courage to be.*

In echoing Tillich, Sidney Jourard summarizes the central message:

> The healthier person will doubtless experience many a bruise for being and disclosing who he is, but he prefers to accept these blows rather than lose himself or sell himself (his authentic being) for short-run acceptability.
>
> Sidney Jourard
> *Disclosing Man to Himself*

Integrity

Modern-day managers are often faced with situations where they are required to commit themselves, either openly or tacitly, to an action they may not agree with. They may be participating, willingly or unwillingly, in activities that are morally and ethically cloudy; questionable from a business point of view; and perhaps of doubtful legality.

John Fendrock
"Crisis of Conscience at Quasar"

⇒✳︎⇐

*L*amar was asked to become the hospital's new president and help solve its financial problems. He quickly found that the hospital did indeed have serious financial problems. But permeating the organization was something more insidious.

The hospital was one of ten in a for-profit corporation. Although located in a middle-class neighborhood and having reasonably modern facilities, it lost between $1 million and $2 million each of the last five years and had become a financial drain on the corporation. The man who had managed the hospital over this five-year period was fired for lack of business acumen.

Now the hospital's corporate officers believed that they had found in Lamar the ideal person to manage the hospital. Lamar had a proven track record not only as a successful hospital administrator, but he also was able to gain the respect of both the administrative staff and the medical doctors wherever he had worked.

Lamar spent the first month on the job getting to know the organization. After some 50 interviews with staff members and medical doctors either one-on-one or in small groups, the new president believed that he had a fair understanding of the inner workings of the hospital.

But what troubled him about the interviews was what was left unsaid. After covering surface issues, Lamar would begin to probe deeper with his questions. And when he did, a number of the individuals became uncomfortable and non-communicative. At that point, more information came from their body language than their words.

Lamar then had follow-up meetings with those individuals whom he believed to be the most candid with him. He found one person in particular who was willing to answer all his questions. Martha was manager of the pharmacy and had 20 years of service with the hospital. Being 64 years of age and having only one year to go until retirement, Martha felt secure in her job—and in her person.

Martha described in some detail the lack of ethics that began five years ago, when Lamar's predecessor assumed the position of president of the hospital. From then on, things went downhill.

Armed with a better compass, Lamar proceeded with his inquiry.

He conducted a number of in-depth interviews with staff. He did not want hearsay or innuendoes; he wanted facts. After examining numerous hospital records and checking and double-checking, he had the information that he was seeking.

Lamar was appalled and disheartened by the results of his inquiry. For example:

1. Patients were being billed on the basis of their ability to pay.

2. Medicare and Medicaid claims were frequently "adjusted" to generate additional revenue for the hospital.

3. Patients' medical records were frequently altered to extend the coverage under Medicare or Medicaid.

4. Several of the medical doctors were known to order specific high-priced surgery based primarily on the patient's ability to pay for the surgery—not on the actual needs of the patient.

5. The education department allowed doctors to enroll in continuing education courses and receive formal credit without actually attending the courses.

6. Theft of food and supplies by workers on the night shift was fairly common—but went unreported.

7. The head of the purchasing department relied almost exclusively on several vendors who were his personal friends.

8. The accounting and finance department apparently kept two sets of books—one for the hospital and one for the government auditors.

9. Staff were "free and easy" in completing their travel expense reports, which were seldom reviewed.

As Lamar reflected on the list of ethical issues, he thought to himself: "My predecessor was fired for his lack of *business* acumen. He should have been fired for his lack of *ethical* acumen. Peter Drucker was indeed correct when he said, 'A tree rots from its top.'"

Lamar knew that he had to confront the staff with his findings. Planning for the meeting was now his number one priority.

Lamar announced a meeting for all hospital staff and doctors. To accommodate staff working second and third shift and the doctors who might have schedule conflicts, he arranged to conduct the same meeting at three different times.

Everyone in attendance will long remember Lamar's famous "Pyramid" speech. This is the gist of what he said:

"I thank you for joining me here. This may be the most important speech that I will ever give as president of your hospital. What I have to say is important and urgent. Please give me your undivided attention.

"What you see on the screen is a pyramid. The pyramid has four sides and a foundation. Each of the five aspects is an integral part of the total pyramid. Remove any one of them and you would not have a pyramid.

"This pyramid represents our hospital. The four sides symbolize our four primary goals and the base symbolizes our principal value. The first side represents our most important goal: Quality Health Care. This is our reason for existence. The second side represents our next most important goal: Self-fulfillment for Staff. We want to provide a challenging and enriching environment that will meet the needs and aspirations of our staff. The next side represents our third goal: to be a Responsible Community Citizen. We want to be recognized in the local community as a responsive medical center, a vital part of the community. And the fourth side represents our last goal: Sound Financial Performance. We want to provide our stockholders a reasonable return on their investment. These are our four goals—and they are listed in order of importance.

"Now I turn to the base of the pyramid, which represents our principal value. That value is Integrity. By 'integrity' I mean basic honesty in dealing with other people. Integrity means doing what is right rather than what is expedient. Without integrity, there will be no trust. And without trust, there will be no cement to hold the pyramid together. That is why I position integrity at the base of the pyramid. Without integrity, the pyramid will collapse.

"In these first six weeks as the new president of your hospital, I have spent most of my time studying the pyramid. I have found that our most critical problem is located in the base of the pyramid. An acidic substance has seeped into the foundation and caused considerable corrosion. And I want to tell you, my friends, that if we don't stop the seepage immediately, the entire pyramid will collapse. This is our most urgent problem.

"I call on you today to join me in helping to rebuild the pyramid. Together, working as a team, I am confident that we can reconstruct the pyramid. No single person can do it alone. But, working together, I am confident that we can do it.

"So I ask each of you to consider very carefully this question: Will you be a pyramid *destroyer* or a pyramid *builder*? If you choose the former, I urge you to depart immediately—without delay. But if you choose the latter, which I sincerely hope that you will, then I beseech you to join me in this most challenging endeavor."

That is what the president said. During his brief presentation, Lamar had the undivided attention of everyone in the room. When he finished, you could have heard a pin drop. This was a very sobering experience for everyone there. And it was clear that each member of the hospital staff was given a choice: to either "get on board" and help reconstruct the pyramid or "get out." No ambiguity here.

Lamar then proceeded to establish an ethics task force comprised of senior administrative staff and medical doctors, with himself serving as task force leader. Within six months, these were some of the significant accomplishments:

- a written code of conduct for the hospital at large
- a written code of conduct tailored to each department, with the department head responsible for assuring compliance with the code of conduct
- a one-day ethics seminar for all members of each department
- a two-hour ethics orientation program for all new employees
- establishment of "ethical issues" as an agenda item for department staff meetings
- a monthly Ethics Bulletin issued to all staff and medical doctors highlighting ethical incidents that had occurred in the hospital and how they were dealt with in an exemplary manner.

With this ethics program in place and the hospital president's constancy of purpose, one began to notice a significant change in the behavior of the staff and the medical doctors. No longer were they doing what was expedient; rather, in most cases, they were doing what was right. The base of the pyramid was being reconstructed. And, in turn, the entire pyramid was becoming more robust.

The question frequently arises: Can a leader teach people to be ethical? Tough call. Can a leader change the behavior of people? Yes. And if this change in behavior endures for an extended period of time, might there then be a change in attitude? Very likely.

This story is a testimony to ethical leadership. What Lamar accomplished was to lift the staff to their higher selves. He was able to get them to focus on higher level values—and to live by those values. This change in ethical conduct will be the legacy that Lamar leaves the hospital.

> The leader is responsible for the set of ethics or norms that govern the behavior of people in the organization. Leaders set the moral tone by choosing carefully the people with whom they surround themselves, by communicating a sense of purpose for the organization, by reinforcing appropriate behaviors, and by articulating these moral positions to internal and external constituencies.
>
> Warren Bennis and Burt Nanus
> *Leaders*

SUMMING UP

*I*n describing the model leader, our basic assumption is that the model leader is, first and foremost, a fully functioning person. The corollary to this assumption is that the fully functioning person possesses five essential faculties: reasoning, coping, knowing, believing, and being, all of which are developed into a real unity. These faculties are translated into five leadership dimensions: reason, sources of power, knowing, core leadership functions, and character. These five dimensions are then subdivided into 25 specific leadership competencies. We assume that any person possessing all of these competencies in fair measure is very close to becoming a model leader.

The question then becomes: What should a person do to become a more effective leader? In addressing this central question, we bring the book to a close. And in summarizing *what* to do, Erich Fromm points the way:

> In the art of living, man is both the artist and the object of his art; he is the sculptor *and* the marble; the physician *and* the patient. . . . While it is true that man's productiveness can create material things, works of art, and systems of thought, *by far the most important object of productiveness is man himself.*

> Erich Fromm
> *Man for Himself*

Truly, each human being has considerable freedom in determining what kind of person he or she will become. And it is true that the individual leader has considerable freedom in determining what kind of leader he or she will become. Granted, inhibiting factors may very well deter the desired changes—such as genetic endowment, age-old habits, and system constraints. Nevertheless, each person is still left with considerable freedom to shape his or her own development. The key is *will*—or determination to change.

If you truly have the will to become a more effective leader, then you can do it. Let me suggest you consider—and implement—the following strategy.

1. **Complete the Leadership Agenda in the appendix.** This Leadership Agenda can serve as your plan of action for becoming a more effective leader. It will be your road map for moving from where you now are toward becoming a model leader. It will take several hours to complete. Do it conscientiously.

2. **Discuss the Leadership Agenda with at least one other person.** This person may be your manager, a mentor, a peer, your spouse, or a friend. You want to select a person who will give you candid feedback and whose judgment and advice you respect.

3. **Implement your Leadership Agenda.** Keep the Agenda not in a desk drawer but on top of your desk. Refer to it frequently as you make your plans for the month, the week, and the day.

4. **Review and reflect.** Take a few minutes at the end of each day to reflect on how well you have implemented your Agenda. What did you do that was exceptionally good—that you could be proud of? And what did you do that was not so good—that you are not very proud of? Be honest—and resolve to do better the next time you are confronted with a similar situation.

5. **Adopt this strategy as a *lifelong activity*.** Becoming a more effective leader is not a 12-month project. It is truly a lifelong activity—and perhaps the most exciting and challenging activity in which you will ever be engaged.

In closing, I would like to leave you with a beautiful quotation that captures the central theme of *The Model Leader*. To each and every person who desires to become a more effective leader, here are words of wisdom:

> Wanting to lead and believing that you can lead are only the departure points on the path to leadership. Leadership is an art, a performing art. And in the art of leadership, the artist's instrument is the self. The mastery of the art of leadership comes with the mastery of the self. Ultimately, leadership development is a process of self-development.
>
> James Kouzes and Barry Posner
> *The Leadership Challenge*

APPENDIX

LEADERSHIP
AGENDA

Instructions

Here is an opportunity to translate ideas into action. This Leadership Agenda covers the 25 leadership competencies included in the text. If you will complete the Leadership Agenda—and then implement it— the probability is very high that you will be a more effective leader.

Review and reflect on the key points in each essay that elaborates on a particular leadership competency. Then complete the assignment for that competency in the Leadership Agenda.

Here is a practical suggestion: Create a file in your personal computer for the entire Leadership Agenda. Then treat the Agenda as a "living document" by updating it on a regular basis. The last exercise in the Agenda—Objectives and Action Steps—should be updated at least quarterly.

If you will follow this plan, you will be certain to achieve a considerable return on investment—in your journey to becoming a model leader.

1. Conceptual Skills

The model leader is able to deal with high order abstraction and generalization.

If managing ideas is an important aspect of your work, what can you do to improve this part of your job?

2. Logical Thinking

The model leader is able to apply a systematic approach to problem solving.

Assume that you are leading a group in a problem solving session. What would be your sequence of steps?

3. Creative Thinking

The model leader is able to bring into being imaginative ideas.

Assume that you are leading a group brainstorming session. What would be your "do's and don't's" for the meeting?

4. Holistic Thinking

The model leader is able to grasp the total situation and to understand the relationships between and among the elements.

What would you do to make certain that your team members have the "big picture" in mind when making decisions?

5. Communication

The model leader is able to engage in genuine dialogue with others.

What can you do to promote honest and open two-way communication in your unit?

6. Staff

The model leader has a team of persons who are ready, willing, and able.

What actions can you take to increase the overall capability of your staff?

7. Information

The model leader knows what information is needed to function effectively and where to get the information.

(a) What are the critical success factors for your unit over the next 12-month period?

(b) How will you gauge the status of each of these critical success factors?

8. Networks

The model leader has many personal contacts with whom ideas, information, and resources can be shared.

(a) Who are the key contacts in your present network?

(b) Who else would you like to include in your network of personal contacts?

9. Knowing Oneself

The model leader has a good grasp of his or her own strengths and limitations and actively seeks feedback for personal growth.

(a) What sources of feedback do you now have for gauging your own performance?

(b) What can you do to increase the breadth and depth of this feedback?

10. Knowing the Job

The model leader understands the requirements of the job and how the job contributes to the goals of the larger organization.

(a) What is the mission of your present job?

(b) How does your job add value to the larger organization?

(c) What can you do to increase the value of what you do?

11. Knowing the Organization

The model leader understands the organization's culture and how to get things done effectively and efficiently.

(a) What is the mission of the larger organization of which you are a part?

(b) What is the vision of the organization?

(c) What are the core values of the organization?

12. Knowing the Business One Is In

The model leader understands the external environment sufficiently well to know customers' needs and what is of value to them.

(a) What are the principal needs of your customers or clients?

(b) What can your unit do to better meet these needs?

13. Knowing the World

The model leader understands the world community and how the smaller communities relate to the larger community.

What actions can you take to promote cultural diversity in your unit?

14. Valuing

The model leader has a good grasp of the organization's values and can translate them into practice.

(a) What are the core values of your organizational unit?

(b) How can you translate these values into practice?

15. Visioning

The model leader has a clear mental picture of a desired future for his or her organization or organizational unit.

What is the vision for your unit?

16. Coaching

The model leader helps others develop the knowledge and skills needed for achieving the vision.

How can you help your staff acquire the knowledge and skills needed for achieving the vision?

17. Empowering

The model leader provides staff with the training, resources, and authority needed to enable them to move toward the vision.

How can you empower your staff so they will be better able to work toward the vision?

18. Team Building

The model leader is able to develop a team of people who are dedicated to working collaboratively to achieve the vision.

What can you do to build a team of people who are dedicated to working collaboratively to achieve the vision?

19. Promoting Quality

The model leader achieves a reputation for always meeting or exceeding customer expectations.

(a) How would you define quality performance for your unit?

(b) How would you measure quality performance for your unit?

20. Identity

The model leader has a unified set of values and lives by those values each day.

What are the core values that define who you are as a person?

21. Independence

The model leader is guided primarily by his or her own internal compass.

Suppose that you found yourself as "a minority of one" in discussing an important issue in a group meeting with peers. How would you deal with the situation?

22. Authenticity

The model leader reveals his or her true being to others; the inner self and the outer self are congruent.

Suppose that you have an individual contributor in your unit who desires to become a manager but has appalling human relations skills. How would you deal with the situation?

23. Responsibility

The model leader takes responsibility for his or her decisions and actions and does not blame others.

Suppose that you work for a manager who instructs you to do something that you believe is unethical. What would you do?

24. Courage

The model leader affirms his or her authentic being despite obstacles.

Suppose that your manager is doing something that is creating a major problem for you. What would you do?

25. Integrity

The model leader is guided by a set of moral principles and is recognized by others as a person of integrity.

What actions can you take to promote ethical conduct in your unit?

Objectives and Action Steps

BIBLIOGRAPHY

Ackoff, Russell. *The Art of Problem Solving.* New York: John Wiley & Sons, 1978.

Adair, John. *Great Leaders.* Guildford, Surrey, England: The Talbot Adair Press, 1989.

Allport, Gordon. *Becoming: Basic Considerations for a Psychology of Personality.* New Haven: Yale University Press, 1955.

Anshen, Melvin. "The Management of Ideas." *Harvard Business Review,* July–August, 1969.

Appley, Lawrence. *Formula for Success: A Core Concept in Management.* New York: American Management Associations, 1974.

Appley, Lawrence. *Management in Action: The Art of Getting Things Done Through People.* New York: American Management Associations, 1956.

Appley, Lawrence. *The Management Evolution.* New York: American Management Associations, 1963.

Appley, Lawrence. *Values in Management.* New York: American Management Associations, 1969.

Aristotle. *The Nicomachean Ethics.* Buffalo, New York: Prometheus Books, 1987.

Barnard, Chester. *Functions of the Executive.* Cambridge: Harvard University Press, 1984.

Barnard, Chester. *Organization and Management.* Cambridge, Massachusetts: Harvard University Press, 1948.

Bass, Bernard. "Leadership: Good, Better, Best." *Organizational Dynamics,* Winter 1985.

Bass, Bernard. *Leadership and Performance Beyond Expectations.* New York: The Free Press, 1985.

Bellah, Robert, Richard Madsen, William Sullivan, Ann Swidler, and Steven Tipton. *Habits of the Heart: Individualism and Commitment in American Life.* Berkeley, California: University of California Press, 1985.

Bennis, Warren. *On Becoming a Leader.* Reading, Massachusetts: Addison-Wesley, 1989.

Bennis, Warren (Ed.). *Leaders on Leadership: Interviews with Top Executives,* Boston: *The Harvard Business Review,* 1992.

Bennis, Warren, and Burt Nanus. *Leaders: The Strategies for Taking Charge.* New York: Harper & Row, 1985.

Black, Algernon. "Our Quest for Faith: Is Humanism Enough?" in *The Humanist Alternative,* edited by Paul Kurtz.

Blake, Robert, and Jane Mouton. *The New Managerial Grid.* Houston, Texas: The Gulf Publishing Company, 1978.

Blanchard, Kenneth, and Spencer Johnson. *The One Minute Manager.* New York: William Morrow, 1982.

Block, Peter. *The Empowered Manager: Positive Political Skills at Work.* San Francisco: Jossey-Bass, 1987.

Bok, Sissela. *Lying: Moral Choice in Public and Private Life.* New York: Vintage Books, 1978.

Bonner, Hubert. *On Being Mindful of Man.* New York: Houghton Mifflin Company, 1965.

Bradford, David, and Allan Cohen. *Managing for Excellence.* New York: John Wiley & Sons, 1984.

Bretall, Robert (Ed.). *A Kierkegaard Anthology.* New York: Random House (The Modern Library), 1946.

Bronowski, Jacob. *The Identity of Man.* Garden City, New York: The Natural History Press, 1965.

Brouwer, Paul. "The Power to See Ourselves." *Harvard Business Review,* Nov.–Dec. 1964.

Bruner, Jerome. *On Knowing: Essays for the Left Hand.* London: Oxford University Press, 1979.

Buber, Martin. *A Believing Humanism: My Testament, 1902–1965.* New York: Simon and Schuster, 1967.

Buber, Martin. *Between Man and Man.* Boston: Beacon Press, 1955.

Buber, Martin. *Hasidism and Modern Man.* New York: Harper & Row (Harper Torchbooks), 1966.

Buber, Martin. *Israel and the World: Essays in a Time of Crisis.* New York: Schocken Books, 1963.

Buber, Martin. *On Judaism.* New York: Schocken Books, 1967.

Buber, Martin. *The Legend of the Baal-Shem.* New York: Schocken Books, 1969.

Buber, Martin. *The Origin and Meaning of Hasidism.* New York: Harper & Row (Harper Torchbooks), 1966.

Buber, Martin. *Pointing the Way.* New York: Harper & Row (Harper Torchbooks), 1963.

Buber, Martin. *Tales of the Hasidim* (Later Masters). New York: Schocken Books, 1948.

Buber, Martin. *Ten Rungs: Hasidic Sayings.* New York: Schocken Books, 1962.

Buber, Martin. *Two Types of Faith.* New York: Harper & Row (Harper Torchbooks), 1961.

Buber, Martin. *The Way of Man: According to the Teaching of Hasidism.* New York: The Citadel Press, 1967.

Bugental, J.F.T. (Ed.). *Challenges of Humanistic Psychology*. New York: McGraw-Hill Book Company, 1967.

Bugental, J.F.T. *The Search for Authenticity: An Existential-Analytic Approach to Psychotherapy*. New York: Holt, Rinehart and Winston, 1965.

Bullen, Christine, and John Rockart. *A Primer on Critical Success Factors*. Cambridge, Massachusetts: Sloan School of Management, 1981.

Burns, James MacGregor. *Leadership*. New York: Harper & Row, 1978.

Cadbury, Sir Adrian. "Ethical Managers Make Their Own Rules." *Harvard Business Review*, Sept.–Oct. 1987.

Campbell, Joseph. *The Power of Myth*. New York: Doubleday, 1988.

Cleveland, Harlan. *The Knowledge Executive*. New York: E. P. Dutton, 1985.

Colbert, Bertram. "The Management Information System." *Management Services*, Sept.–Oct. 1967.

Crosby, Philip. *Quality is Free: The Art of Making Quality Certain*. New York: McGraw-Hill Book Company, 1979.

D'Aprix, Roger. *Communicating for Productivity*. New York: Harper & Row, 1982.

Davis, Stanley. *Managing Corporate Culture*. Cambridge, Massachusetts: Ballinger Publishing Company, 1984.

Deal, Terrence, and Allan Kennedy. *Corporate Cultures: The Rites and Rituals of Corporate Life*. Reading, Massachusetts: Addison-Wesley, 1982.

Deming, W. Edwards. *Out of the Crisis*. Cambridge, Massachusetts: Massachusetts Institute of Technology, 1986.

DePree, Max. *Leadership is an Art*. New York: Doubleday, 1989.

Dewey, John. *A Common Faith*. New Haven: Yale University Press, 1934.

Dewey, John. *How We Think*. Boston: D. C. Heath and Company, 1933.

Dowling, William (Ed.). *Effective Management and the Behavioral Sciences*. New York: AMACOM, a division of the American Management Associations, 1978.

Drucker, Peter. *The Effective Executive.* New York: Harper & Row (Harper Colophon Books), 1967.

Drucker, Peter. *Management: Tasks, Responsibilities, Practices.* New York: Harper & Row, 1973.

Drucker, Peter. *Managing for Results.* New York: Harper & Row, 1964.

Drucker, Peter. *Managing in Turbulent Times.* New York: Harper & Row, 1980.

Drucker, Peter. *The New Realities.* New York: Harper & Row, 1989.

Drucker, Peter. *The Practice of Management.* New York: Harper & Row, 1954.

Dyer, William. *Contemporary Issues in Management and Organization Development.* Reading, Massachusetts: Addison-Wesley Publishing Company, 1983.

Dyer, William. *Team Building: Issues and Alternatives.* Reading, Massachusetts: Addison-Wesley Publishing Company, 1977.

Elbing, Alvar, and Carol Elbing. *The Value Issue of Business.* New York: McGraw-Hill Book Company, 1967.

Emerson, Ralph Waldo. *Emerson's Essays.* New York: Thomas Y. Crowell Company, 1926.

Emerson, Ralph Waldo. *Essays and Lectures.* New York: The Library of America, 1983.

Erikson, Erik. *Insight and Responsibility.* New York: W. W. Norton & Company, 1964.

Fadiman, Clifton (ed.). *Living Philosophies: The Reflections of Some Eminant Men and Women of Our Time.* New York: Doubleday, 1990.

Fairley, Barker. *A Study of Goethe.* London: Oxford, 1947.

Fendrock, John. "Crisis of Conscience at Quasar." *Harvard Business Review,* March–April 1968.

Feuerbach, Ludwig. *Principles of the Philosophy of the Future.* New York: The Bobbs-Merrill Company, 1966.

Follett, Mary Parker. *Freedom and Coordination*. London: Pitman, 1949.

Frankl, Viktor. *The Will to Meaning*. Bergenfield, New Jersey: New American Library, 1969.

Freudberg, David. *The Corporate Conscience*. New York: AMACOM, a division of American Management Associations, 1986.

Fromm, Erich. *The Art of Loving*. New York: Harper & Row, 1956.

Fromm, Erich. *Escape from Freedom*. New York: Holt, Rinehart and Winston, 1941.

Fromm, Erich. *To Have Or To Be?* New York, Harper & Row, 1976.

Fromm, Erich. *Man for Himself: An Inquiry into the Psychology of Ethics*. New York: Fawcett World Library, 1947.

Fromm, Erich. *The Revolution of Hope: Toward a Humanized Technology*. New York: Harper & Row (Harper Colophon Books), 1970.

Gardner, John. *Excellence*. New York: W. W. Norton & Company, 1984.

Gardner, John. *On Leadership*. New York: The Free Press, 1990.

Gardner, John. *Morale*. New York: W. W. Norton, 1978.

Gardner, John. *No Easy Victories*. New York: Harper & Row, 1968.

Gardner, John. *Self-Renewal: The Individual and the Innovative Society*. New York: Harper & Row (Harper Colophon Books), 1965.

Garfield, Charles. *Second to None: How Our Smartest Companies Put People First*. Homewood, Illinois: Business One Irwin, 1992.

Gellerman, Saul. *Management by Motivation*. New York: American Management Associations, 1968.

Gellerman, Saul. *Motivation and Productivity*. New York: American Management Associations, 1963.

Geneen, Harold. *Managing*. New York: Doubleday & Company, 1984.

Gerth, H. H., and C. Wright Mills (Eds.). *From Max Weber: Essays in Sociology*. New York: Oxford University Press, 1958.

Giblan, Edward. "The Road to Managerial Wisdom—and How to Get on It." *Management Review*, April 1984.

Gibran, Kahlil. *The Prophet.* New York: Alfred A. Knopf, 1923.

Gibran, Kahlil. *A Second Treasury of Kahlil Gibran.* Secaucus, New Jersey: The Citadel Press, 1962.

Gibran, Kahlil. "The Voice of the Master." In *A Second Treasury of Kahlil Gibran.*

Gilbreath, Robert. "The Hollow Executive." *New Management,* Spring 1987.

Goldratt, Eliyahu, and Jeff Cox. *The Goal: A Process of Ongoing Improvement.* Croton-on-Hudson, N. Y.: North River Press, 1986.

Guth, William, and Renato Tagiuri. "Personal Values and Corporate Strategy." *Harvard Business Review,* Sept.–Oct. 1965.

Hamilton, Edith, and Huntington Cairns (Eds.). *The Collected Dialogues of Plato.* New York: Bollingen Foundation, 1961.

Hammarskjöld, Dag. *Markings.* New York: Alfred A. Knopf, 1966.

Hersey, Paul, and Kenneth Blanchard. *Management of Organizational Behavior.* Englewood Cliffs, N. J.: Prentice-Hall, 1977.

Hodes, Aubrey. *Martin Buber: An Intimate Portrait.* New York: The Viking Press, 1971.

Hodnett, Edward. *The Art of Problem Solving.* New York: Harper & Brothers, 1955.

Holmes, Robert. "Developing Better Management Information Systems." *Financial Executive,* July 1970.

Horton, Thomas. *"What Works for Me": 16 CEOs Talk About Their Careers and Commitments.* New York: Random House, 1986.

Huxley, Julian (Ed.). *The Humanist Frame.* New York: Harper & Row, 1961.

Iacocca, Lee. *Iacocca: An Autobiography.* New York: Bantam Books, 1984.

James, William. *Pragmatism and four essays from The Meaning of Truth.* New York: The World Publishing Company (Meridian Books), 1955.

James, William. *The Principles of Psychology I.* New York: Dover Publications, 1950.

James, William. *Some Problems in Philosophy.* New York: Longman's Green and Company, 1911.

James, William. *The Will to Believe and Other Essays on Popular Philosophy.* New York: Dover Publications, 1956.

Janis, Irving. *Groupthink.* Boston: Houghton Mifflin, 1982.

Jaspers, Karl. *The Future of Mankind.* Chicago: The University of Chicago Press, 1961.

Jaspers, Karl. *General Psychopathology.* Chicago: The University of Chicago Press, 1963.

Jaspers, Karl. *The Great Philosophers I.* New York: Harcourt Brace Jovanovich, 1962.

Jaspers, Karl. *Man in the Modern Age.* Garden City, New York: Doubleday & Company (Doubleday Anchor Books), 1957.

Jaspers, Karl. *Philosophical Faith and Revelation.* New York: Harper & Row, 1967.

Jaspers, Karl. *Philosophy I.* Chicago: The University of Chicago Press, 1969.

Jaspers, Karl. *Philosophy II.* Chicago: The University of Chicago Press, 1970.

Jaspers, Karl. *Philosophy is for Everyman.* New York: Harcourt Brace Jovanovich, 1967.

Jaspers, Karl. *Philosophy of Existence.* Philadelphia: University of Pennsylvania Press, 1971.

Jaspers, Karl. *Reason and Anti-Reason in Our Time.* New Haven: Yale University Press, 1952.

Jaspers, Karl. *Reason and Existenz.* New York: The Noonday Press, 1955.

Jaspers, Karl. *Three Essays: Leonardo, Descartes, Max Weber.* New York: Harcourt Brace Jovanovich, 1964.

Jaspers, Karl. *Way to Wisdom.* New Haven: Yale University Press, 1954.

Jenkins, James, and Donald Paterson (Eds.). *Studies in Individual Differences: The Search for Intelligence*. New York: Appleton-Century-Crofts, 1961.

Josephson, Michael. Quoted in "Ethics: Looking at Its Roots," by Ezra Bowen. *Time*, May 25, 1987.

Jourard, Sidney. *Disclosing Man to Himself*. New York: VanNostrand Reinhold Company, 1968.

Jourard, Sidney. *Healthy Personality: An Approach from the Viewpoint of Humanistic Psychology*. New York: Macmillan Publishing Company, 1974.

Jowett, B. (Ed.). *The Dialogues of Plato*. New York: Random House, 1920.

Kant, Immanuel. *Critique of Pure Reason*. New York: Random House (The Modern Library), 1958.

Kant, Immanuel. *On History*. New York: The Bobbs-Merrill Company, 1963.

Kant, Immanuel. *Lectures on Ethics*. New York: Harper & Row, 1963.

Kant, Immanuel. *Religion Within the Limits of Reason Alone*. New York: Harper & Row (Harper Torchbooks), 1960.

Kanter, Rosabeth Moss. *The Change Masters*. New York: Simon and Schuster, 1983.

Kanter, Rosabeth Moss. *When Giants Learn to Dance: Mastering the Challenges of Strategy, Management, and Careers in the 1990s*. New York: Simon and Schuster, 1989.

Katz, Daniel, and Robert Kahn. *The Social Psychology of Organizations*. New York: John Wiley & Sons, 1978.

Kaufmann, Walter. *Basic Writings of Nietzsche*. New York: Random House (The Modern Library), 1968.

Kelen, Emery (Ed.) *Hammarskjöld: The Political Man*. New York: Funk & Wagnalls Publishing Company, 1968.

Kelly, George. *A Theory of Personality: The Psychology of Personal Constructs*. New York: W. W. Norton & Company, 1963.

Kepner, Charles, and Benjamin Tregoe. "Developing Decision Makers." *Harvard Business Review*, Sept.–Oct. 1960.

Kepner, Charles, and Benjamin Tregoe. *The Rational Manager*. New York: McGraw-Hill Book Company, 1965.

Kierkegaard, Sören. *Purity of Heart is to Will One Thing*. New York: Harper & Row (Harper Torchbooks), 1956.

Kierkegaard, Sören. *The Sickness Unto Death*. (In *Fear and Trembling and The Sickness Unto Death*). Princeton, New Jersey: Princeton University Press, 1954.

Kinget, E. Marian. *On Being Human: A Systematic View*. New York: Harcourt Brace Jovanovich, 1975.

Knight, Margaret (Ed.). *Humanist Anthology*. London: Pemberton Publishing Company, 1961.

Koch, Adrienne, and William Penden (eds). *The Life and Selected Writings of Thomas Jefferson*. New York: Random House (Modern Library), 1944.

Koontz, Harold, Cyril O'Donnell, and Heinz Weihrich. *Management*. New York: McGraw-Hill Book Company, 1980.

Kotter, John. *A Force for Change: How Leadership Differs from Management*. New York: The Free Press, 1990.

Kotter, John. *The Leadership Factor*. New York: The Free Press, 1988.

Kouzes, James, and Barry Posner. The Leadership Challenge. San Francisco: Jossey-Bass, 1987.

Kurtz, Paul. *The Fullness of Life*. New York: Horizon Press, 1974.

Kurtz, Paul (Ed.). *The Humanist Alternative: Some Definitions of Humanism*. Buffalo, New York: Prometheus Books, 1973.

Landen, Delmar, and Howard Carlson. "New Strategies for Motivating Employees." In *The Failure of Success*, edited by Alfred Marrow.

Levinson, Harry. "Asinine Attitudes Toward Motivation." *Harvard Business Review*, Jan.–Feb. 1973.

Levinson, Harry. "Management by Whose Objectives?" *Harvard Business Review*, July–August 1970.

Likert, Rensis. *The Human Organization: Its Management and Value.* New York: McGraw-Hill Book Company, 1967.

Likert, Rensis. *New Patterns of Management.* New York: McGraw-Hill Book Company, 1961.

Lin, Yutang (Ed.). *The Wisdom of Confucius.* New York: Random House (The Modern Library), 1938.

Lipnack, Jessica, and Jeffrey Stamps. *Networking.* Garden City, New York: Doubleday, 1982.

Lippitt, Gordon. *Organization Renewal: Achieving Viability in a Changing World.* New York: Meredith Corporation, 1969.

Livingston, Sterling. "Pygmalion in Management." *Harvard Business Review,* July–August 1969.

Machiavelli, Niccolò. *The Prince.* New York: The New American Library, 1980.

Maier, Norman. *The Appraisal Interview: Three Basic Approaches.* La-Jolla, California: University Associates, 1976.

Maier, Norman. *Problem-Solving Discussions and Conferences: Leadership Methods and Skills.* New York: McGraw-Hill Book Company, 1963.

Marcel, Gabriel. *The Philosophy of Existentialism.* New York: The Citadel Press, 1956.

Marrow, Alfred (Ed.). *The Failure of Success.* New York: American Management Associations, 1972.

Maslow, Abraham. *Eupsychian Management.* Homewood, Illinois: Richard D. Irwin, 1965.

Maslow, Abraham. *The Farther Reaches of Human Nature.* New York: The Viking Press, 1971.

Maslow, Abraham. *Motivation and Personality.* New York: Harper & Row, 1970.

Maslow, Abraham. "Self-Actualizing and Beyond." In *Challenges of Humanistic Psychology,* edited by J.F.T. Bugental.

Maslow, Abraham. "Synanon and Eupsychia." *Journal of Humanistic Psychology,* 7, 1967.

Maslow, Abraham. *Toward a Psychology of Being.* New York: VanNostrand Reinhold Company, 1968.

Maslow, Bertha (Ed.). *Abraham Maslow: A Memorial Volume.* Monterey, California: Brooks/Cole Publishing Company, 1972.

May, Rollo. *The Courage to Create.* New York: Bantam Books, 1975.

May, Rollo. *Love and Will.* New York: W. W. Norton & Company, 1969.

May, Rollo. *Man's Search for Himself.* New York: Dell Publishing Company, 1953.

May, Rollo. *Psychology and the Human Dilemma.* New York: VanNostrand Reinhold Company, 1967.

McCall, Morgan, Michael Lombardo, and Ann Morrison. *The Lessons of Experience: How Successful Executives Develop on the Job.* Lexington, Mass.: Lexington Book, 1988.

McCormack, Mark. *What They Don't Teach You at Harvard Business School.* New York: Bantam Books, 1984.

McGregor, Douglas. *The Human Side of Enterprise.* New York: McGraw-Hill Book Company. 1960.

McGregor, Douglas. *The Professional Manager.* New York: McGraw-Hill Book Company, 1967.

Mill, John Stuart. *On Liberty.* New York: The Bobbs-Merrill Company, 1956.

Miller, Samuel. "The Tangle of Ethics." *Harvard Business Review,* Jan.–Feb. 1960.

Mintzberg, Henry. "The Manager's Job." *Harvard Business Review,* July–August 1975.

Mintzberg, Henry. *The Nature of Managerial Work.* Englewood Cliffs, New Jersey: Prentice-Hall, 1980.

Moran, Lord. *The Anatomy of Courage.* London: Constable, 1945.

Moustakas, Clark. "Explorations in Essential Being." In *The Self: Explorations in Personal Growth*, edited by Clark Moustakas.

Moustakas, Clark. *Loneliness and Love.* Englewood Cliffs, New Jersey: Prentice-Hall (A Spectrum Book), 1972.

Moustakas, Clark (Ed.). *The Self: Explorations in Personal Growth.* New York: Harper & Row, 1956.

Moyers, Bill. *A World of Ideas.* New York: Doubleday, 1989.

Murphy, Gardner. *Human Potentialities.* New York: Basic Books, 1958.

Naisbitt, John. *Megatrends: Ten New Directions Transforming Our Lives.* New York: Warner Books, 1982.

Ohmann, O. A. "Skyhooks." *Harvard Business Review*, May–June 1955.

Owen, Robert. *A New View of Society.* New York: E. Bliss & E. White, 1825.

Pascale, Richard, and Anthony Athos. *The Art of Japanese Management: Applications for American Executives.* New York: Simon and Schuster, 1981.

Pastin, Mark. "Ethics and Excellence." *New Management*, Spring 1987.

Pastin, Mark. *The Hard Problems of Management: Gaining the Ethics Edge.* San Francisco: Jossey-Bass, 1986.

Peck, M. Scott. *The Road Less Traveled.* New York: Simon and Schuster, 1978.

Peters, Thomas, and Robert Waterman. *In Search of Excellence: Lessons from America's Best-Run Companies.* New York: Harper & Row, 1982.

Peters, Tom, and Nancy Austin. *A Passion for Excellence: The Leadership Difference.* New York: Random House, 1985.

Platt, John Rader. *The Step to Man.* New York: John Wiley & Sons, 1966.

Polanyi, Michael. *Personal Knowledge: Towards a Post-Critical Philosophy.* New York: Harper & Row (Harper Torchbooks), 1964.

Polanyi, Michael. *The Study of Man.* Chicago: The University of Chicago Press (Phoenix Books), 1963.

Powell, General Colin. Address to the graduating class at Fisk University. Reported in the *Columbus Dispatch,* May 13, 1992.

Quinn, James Brian. *Strategies for Change: Logical Incrementalism.* Homewood, Illinois: Richard D. Irwin, 1980.

Quotations from Our Presidents. Mount Vernon, New York: Peter Pauper Press, 1969.

Riesman, David. *The Lonely Crowd.* New Haven: Yale University Press, 1961.

Roethlisberger, Fritz. "The Human Equation in Employee Productivity." Speech before the Personnel Group of the National Retail Dry Goods Association, 1950.

Rogers, Carl. *On Becoming a Person.* Boston: Houghton Mifflin Company (Sentry Edition), 1961.

Rogers, Carl, and F. J. Roethlisberger. "Barriers and Gateways to Communication." *Harvard Business Review,* July–August 1952.

Rokeach, Milton. *The Nature of Human Values.* New York: The Free Press, 1973.

Russell, Bertrand. *The Art of Philosophizing and Other Essays.* Totowa, New Jersey: Littlefield, Adams & Company, 1974.

Russell, Bertrand. *Education and the Good Life.* New York: Liveright Publishing Corporation, 1970.

Russell, Bertrand. *New Hopes for a Changing World.* New York: Minerva Books, 1951.

Russell, Bertrand. *Unpopular Essays.* New York: Simon and Schuster (A Touchstone Book), 1950.

Sashkin, Marshall. *A Manager's Guide to Participative Management.* New York: American Management Associations, 1982.

Schilpp, Paul Arthur (Ed.). *The Philosophy of Karl Jaspers.* New York: Tudor Publishing Company, 1957.

Schilpp, Paul Arthur, and Maurice Friedman (Eds.). *The Philosophy of Martin Buber.* La Salle, Illinois: The Open Court Publishing Co., 1967.

Senge, Peter. *The Fifth Discipline: The Art & Practice of the Learning Organization.* New York: Doubleday/Currency, 1990.

Shea, Gordon. *Building Trust in the Workplace.* New York: American Management Associations, 1984.

Solomon, Robert, and Kristine Hanson. *Above the Bottom Line: An Introduction to Business Ethics.* New York: Harcourt Brace Jovanovich, 1983.

Srivastva, Suresh, and Associates. *Executive Integrity: The Search for High Human Values in Organizational Life.* San Francisco: Jossey-Bass, 1988.

Swift, Marvin. "Clear Writing Means Clear Thinking Means . . ." *Harvard Business Review,* Jan.–Feb. 1973.

Tagore, Rabindranath. *Personality.* New York: Macmillan Publishing Company, 1918.

Taylor, Frederick. *Scientific Management.* Hanover, N. H.: Dartmouth College, 1912.

Tichy, Noel, and Ram Charan. "Speed, Simplicity, Self-Confidence: An Interview with Jack Welch." *Harvard Business Review,* Sept.–Oct. 1989.

Tillich, Paul. *Biblical Religion and the Search for Ultimate Reality.* Chicago: The University of Chicago Press (Phoenix Books), 1955.

Tillich, Paul. *The Courage To Be.* New Haven: Yale University Press, 1952.

Tillich, Paul. *Dynamics of Faith.* New York: Harper & Row (Harper Torchbooks), 1958.

Tillich, Paul. *The Eternal Now.* New York: Charles Scribner's Sons, 1956.

Tillich, Paul. *Morality and Beyond.* New York: Harper & Row, 1963.

Tillich, Paul. *The New Being.* New York: Charles Scribner's Sons, 1955.

Tillich, Paul. *The Shaking of the Foundations.* New York: Charles Scribner's Sons, 1948.

Tournier, Paul. *The Meaning of Persons.* New York: Harper & Row, 1957.

Tyler, Leona. *The Psychology of Human Differences.* New York: Appleton-Century-Crofts, 1956.

Urwick, Lyndall. "Scientific Principles and Organization." Institute of Management Series No. 19, American Management Associations, 1938.

Weber, Max. *The Theory of Social and Economic Organization*. New York: The Crowell-Collier Publishing Company, 1947.

Weinstein, Joshua. *Buber and Humanistic Education*. New York: Philosophical Library, 1975.

Wheelis, Allen. *The Quest for Identity*. New York: W. W. Norton & Company, 1958.

Whyte, William H. Jr. *The Organization Man*. New York: Simon and Schuster, 1956.

Williams, Bernard. *Ethics and the Limits of Philosophy*. Cambridge, Massachusetts: Harvard University Press, 1985.

Wilson, Francis. "Human Nature and Aesthetic Growth." In *The Self*, edited by Clark Moustakas.

Woodworth, Robert, and Harold Schlosberg. *Experimental Psychology*. New York: Henry Holt and Company, 1954.

Zaleznik, Abraham. "The Human Dilemmas of Leadership." *Harvard Business Review*, July–August 1963.

Zaleznik, Abraham. *The Managerial Mystique: Restoring Leadership in Business*. New York: Harper & Row, 1989.

Zaleznik, Abraham. "Managers and Leaders: Are They Different?" *Harvard Business Review*, May–June 1977.

AUTHOR INDEX

SUBJECT INDEX